Developing
Reading-Writing
Connections

Strategies From The Reading Teacher

Timothy V. Rasinski

Nancy D. Padak

Brenda Weible Church

Gay Fawcett

Judith Hendershot

Justina M. Henry

Barbara G. Moss

Jacqueline K. Peck

Elizabeth (Betsy) Pryor

Kathleen A. Roskos

Editors

x

INTERNATIONAL
Reading
®**Association**

800 Barksdale Road, PO Box 8139
Newark, Delaware 19714-8139, USA
www.reading.org

The International Reading Association attempts, through its publications, to provide a forum for a wide spectrum of opinions on reading. This policy permits divergent viewpoints without implying the endorsement of the Association.

Director of Publications   Joan M. Irwin
Editorial Director, Books and Special Projects   Matthew W. Baker
Special Projects Editor   Tori Mello Bachman
Permissions Editor   Janet S. Parrack
Associate Editor   Jeanine K. McGann
Production Editor   Shannon Benner
Editorial Assistant   Pamela McComas
Publications Coordinator   Beth Doughty
Production Department Manager   Iona Sauscermen
Art Director   Boni Nash
Senior Electronic Publishing Specialist   Anette Schütz-Ruff
Electronic Publishing Specialist   Cheryl J. Strum
Electronic Publishing Assistant   John W. Cain

Library of Congress Cataloging-in-Publication Data
Developing reading-writing connections : strategies from The reading teacher / Timothy Rasinski ... [et al.], editors.
     p.   cm.
   Includes bibliographical references.
ISBN 0-87207-280-0
    1. Reading (Elementary)   2. Language arts (Elementary)   3. Children's literature—Study and teaching (Elementary)   I. Rasinski, Timothy V.   II. Reading teacher.
LB1573.D44   2000
372.4—dc21
                                                                            00-058196

Contents

About the editors

Timothy V. Rasinski
Professor of Education
Kent State University
Kent, Ohio, USA

Nancy D. Padak
Professor, Education; Director, Reading
  & Writing Center
Kent State University
Kent, Ohio, USA

Brenda Weible Church
Principal of Seiberling Elementary
  School
Akron Public Schools
Akron, Ohio, USA

Gay Fawcett
Executive Director of the Research
  Center for Educational Technology
Kent State University
Kent, Ohio, USA

Judith Hendershot
Teacher
Field Local Schools
Mogadore, Ohio, USA

Justina M. Henry
Literacy Collaborative-Project Trainer
The Ohio State University
Columbus, Ohio, USA

Barbara G. Moss
Research Associate
CASAS
San Diego, California, USA

Jacqueline K. Peck
PT3 Project Director
Kent State University
Kent, Ohio, USA

Elizabeth (Betsy) Pryor
Educational consultant; retired as super-
  visor of K–12 Reading/Language Arts
  for Columbus Public Schools
Worthington, Ohio, USA

Kathleen A. Roskos
Professor
John Carroll University
University Heights, Ohio, USA

Introduction

Only within the past 25 years or so have we come to acknowledge in the field of literacy education the critical role that children's literature plays in any reading program. It is through the wonderful books and other reading material available for children that they apply the strategies and skills they learn in their reading instruction. It is through reading authentic texts in elementary school that children develop a love of reading that will carry them into lifelong reading.

We have come to these understandings through observing expert teachers turn on their students to reading through sharing with them the best books and other print material that is available. However, even more recently, empirical research has demonstrated that literature for children plays an integral role in their literacy development. Simply providing students with access to authentic literature through book floods increases students' comprehension and overall reading proficiency (Smith & Elley, 1997). And, in a large-scale international study of reading education, teachers' emphasis on literature and their provision of easy access to authentic literature were shown to be significantly associated with student achievement in reading (Postlethwaite & Ross, 1992).

Using literature in the classroom yields rich rewards. Children in literature-based classrooms have more positive attitudes toward reading and value reading more than children in traditional programs (Cullinan, Jagger, & Strickland, 1974). Literature benefits children's language development (Tunnell & Jacobs, 1989). Children who are exposed to literature exhibit greater appreciation for language and illustration and are better able to select books appropriate to their age and interests (Hennings, 1986). Listening to literature read aloud allows children to internalize the language of books and begin to use it in their own oral and written language. As children develop an increased sense of story by reading and talking about books, they reveal that understanding in their own writing. They demonstrate a greater knowledge of how authors combine literary elements such as characters, setting, and plot to create vivid stories.

Thus, the role of authentic and appropriate literature for children is being recognized as increasingly important in children's reading development. At the same time, reading scholars have been informing us about the importance of writing in students' reading development and the importance of reading in children's development as writers. The reading-writing connection is clear and needs to be emphasized in all elementary classrooms.

Reading and writing inform and improve each other—the more students write, the better their reading will become. The more students read, the better their writing will become. As students write and begin to believe in themselves as real writers for real purposes, they will read more widely and deeply (Silvers, 1986). And, reading with the eyes of a writer helps students see what it takes to make engaging and accessible texts for a wide variety of readers.

With *Developing Reading-Writing Connections*, one of four books in the Teaching Reading Collection, we share with you classroom-tested ideas and approaches for helping teachers make literature and writing integral and effective parts of any reading program. The articles have been drawn primarily from the Teaching Reading department of *The Reading Teacher* during our 6-year tenure as editors; this section of the journal is devoted to practical reading instruction strategies for classrooms, reading clinics, and homes. The ideas and support materials included in this book are examples of authentic and thoughtful classroom practice. The contributors subscribe to a broad understanding of the importance of literacy learning: That literacy is central to all learning and that literacy is learned through the work of dedicated and caring teachers at every grade level. The purpose of this book, then, is to present teacher-tested ideas, resources, and activities to develop the reading-writing connection for students and teachers involved in the learning and teaching of reading.

The articles in this volume were submitted to *The Reading Teacher* by teachers from around the world as examples of best and innovative practice in their classrooms. During our editorship we received thousands of articles of this type, but only a select few were chosen for publication in the journal. Each article went through a review process that consisted of at least three separate readings and rankings. Only those that were given the highest ratings were actually published. For this present volume, we examined again those articles that appeared in *RT*. Again we read and rated them, primarily for clarity, purpose, adherence to a particular theme, ease of implementation, and adaptability in a variety of classroom and other educational settings. Only those articles that met these high standards and criteria were chosen for this volume. In this volume you are reading the "best of the best" of practical literature and writing strategies from *The Reading Teacher*.

The ideas and strategies offered in this volume can be used to enliven nearly any reading program. We challenge you, as you read this book, to integrate the instructional ideas you find most appropriate for your own instructional programs. For many students, these ideas may be the spark that makes reading the vehicle for inspiration and imagination that it was meant to be.

We have enjoyed our collaboration with this book's contributors, who are practitioners and experts, and we have come to appreciate the tireless work of dedicated and selfless reading teachers around the world. We hope that you, teachers and teacher educators, will find this book helpful, supportive, and energizing as we all work toward a fully literate global society.

TR, NP, JH, BM,
BC, GF, TH,
JP, BP, KR

REFERENCES

Cullinan, B.E., Jagger, A., & Strickland, D. (1974). Language expansion for black children in primary grades: A research report. *Young Children, 29*, 98–112.

Hennings, D.G. (1986). *Communication in action: Teaching the language arts* (3rd ed.). Boston: Houghton Mifflin.

Postlethwaite, T.N., & Ross, K.N. (1992). *Effective schools in reading: Implications for educational planners*. The Hague: International Association for the Evaluation of Educational Achievement.

Silvers, P. (1986). Process writing and the reading connection. *The Reading Teacher, 39*, 684–688.

Smith, J., & Elley, W. (1997). *How children learn to read*. Katonah, NY: Richard C. Owen.

Tunnell, M.O., & Jacobs, J.S. (1989). Using "real" books: Research findings on literature-based reading instruction. *The Reading Teacher, 42*, 470–477.

A checklist for choosing nonfiction trade books

Peg Sudol
Caryn M. King

VOLUME 49, NUMBER 5, FEBRUARY 1996

Many teachers are using trade books to teach language arts and content area subjects. Although fiction has been the most popular genre, nonfiction trade books are also widely available. One problem, however, is finding appropriate content-related trade books. As Richards (1994) points out, "Almost overnight teachers have been asked to become children's literature experts, knowing the perfect book for every situation, every reader, every curriculum area" (p. 90).

We've had to deal with this problem when locating science trade books for a research project. Based on our work we would like to offer some tips and guidelines for choosing nonfiction. We found *Books in Print*, *Book Review Digest*, and *Book Review Index* helpful. Book jobbers have also been accommodating. Most jobbers have toll-free telephone numbers and send free catalogs to interested teachers. We used Baker and Taylor, Follett, and Libraries Unlimited. We also checked periodicals such as *School Library Journal*, *Booklist*, *Childhood Education*, and *Horn Book Guide*. Since we were looking for nonfiction trade books to use in science classrooms, we also consulted *Appraisal Science Books for Young Children*, *Science Books and Films*, and *Science and Children*. All of these sources were in our university library.

Once we located nonfiction trade books, we faced a more daunting problem: how to select good ones. Consequently, we developed a checklist. We believe this checklist can be especially useful for busy classroom teachers who need a quick and efficient method for reviewing and evaluating trade books, and who, like us, have limited funds.

We looked at a number of resources when designing our checklist. We used Vacca and Vacca's (1993) adaptation of the Irwin and Davis (1980) Readability Checklist and Armbruster and Anderson's (1981) concept of considerate texts. For additional ideas, we consulted Burke

4

and Glazer's (1994) *Using Nonfiction in the Classroom*.

The first section of our checklist is *accuracy*. Often teachers do not take the time to think about a book's accuracy. We assume that if the information is on the page, it is accurate. Yet that is not always the case. To check for accuracy, we ask these questions: Is information on the author's experience and expertise provided? Are photo credits included? Are references cited throughout the text or included in a bibliography? And, of course, is the information current (Burke & Glazer, 1994)?

The second section of our checklist is *organization and layout*. This section examines if the text is arranged in a way that makes it easy to read and use. For example, is there a table of contents that gives an overview of the book's contents? Do chapter and section headings provide information about the important concepts (Armbruster & Anderson, 1981)? Do an index and glossary aid the reader in finding specific information? Are visual aids such as charts, graphs, maps, and illustrations used to assist the reader's comprehension (Vacca & Vacca, 1993)?

Moreover, because well-written nonfiction should be organized to allow the reader to see relationships among concepts, this section also looks at the predominant pattern of organization—cause and effect, comparison/contrast, problem/solution, time order, or description. We ask, "Is this pattern the most appropriate way to explain the concepts?"

The third section of our checklist is *cohesion of ideas*. In cohesive text, ideas are unified and logically ordered from beginning to end. Both unity and coherence are vital within individual paragraphs as well as throughout the text. Unity within a paragraph occurs when the text includes words or phrases that signal connections explicitly (i.e., *because, therefore, as a result*) so that the reader does not have to make too many inferential leaps between ideas. Unity of the whole text occurs when all ideas belong together and develop the thesis statement.

Another concern is whether or not the text respects the reader's background knowledge. Does the reader know enough to make the necessary connections, or does the author assume the reader has more prior knowledge than is likely (Armbruster & Anderson, 1981)? An appropriate conceptual load is important as well. Are abstract concepts introduced one at a time and accompanied by a sufficient number of concrete, relevant examples (Vacca & Vacca, 1993), or does the author include irrelevant details? In general, is the text a good model of expository writing?

The fourth section of our checklist is *specialized vocabulary*. By necessity, nonfiction contains much technical vocabulary. Typically, nonfiction trade books define vocabulary in one of three ways: (a) the text may define special words as they are introduced; (b) pictures with captions or labels may define and clarify the vocabulary; (c) a glossary may give definitions for technical terms (Burke & Glazer, 1994). In each of these cases, the vocabulary needs to be explained in a way the reader can understand, at a lower

A checklist for evaluating nonfiction trade books

Theme: _____ Price: _____
Author: _____ Call no.:_____
Title: _____
Publisher and date: _____
Series: _____ ISBN: _____
Total score: _____ Recommend? _____ For whom? _____

3 = meets all or most criteria   **2** = meets some criteria   **1** = meets few criteria

Check all that apply, or write NA if not applicable. Then select an overall score for each category.

_____ **Accuracy**
     information about author expertise/experience given
     information about photo credits given
     references cited throughout text or bibliography provided
     information is current and accurate

_____ **Organization & layout**

table of contents	chapter and section headings	summaries
index	glossary	charts
graphs	maps	illustrations

     predominant pattern of organization: cause & effect, comparison/contrast, problem/solution, time order, description

_____ **Cohesion of ideas**
     major ideas are logically connected throughout text
     sentence level ideas are logically connected to each other
       (i.e., do not require reader to make a lot of inferences)
     respects reader's probable background knowledge
     appropriate conceptual load
     avoids irrelevant details
     provides good model of expository writing

_____ **Specialized vocabulary**
     defined as it is introduced
     defined in pictures, captions, labels, or clarified visually
     defined in glossary

_____ **Reader interest**
     has aesthetic appeal
     has colorful illustrations or photos
     uses appropriate format (i.e., page and print size)
     has positive role models with respect to gender and ethnicity
     activities and/or experiments within the text are motivating

Annotation:

level of abstraction than the word being defined (Vacca & Vacca, 1993).

The fifth section of our checklist is *reader interest*. Quite simply, we want to know if the text grabs and holds the reader's attention. We ask, "Is the text visually attractive? Does it include colorful illustrations or photos? Is the format appropriate (page and print size)? Are positive gender and racial/ethnic role models provided? Will the students be excited by the activities and experiments described? Will they want to read the text?"

After completing the checklist, we find it helpful to write a short annotation. Usually we list the major concepts that the book addresses. Then we note any unusual or outstanding features. The annotation is especially handy when reviewing many books on the same topic.

So far, we have used this checklist to evaluate dozens of science trade books. The process does not take very long, and when we finish filling out the checklist, we are able to decide quickly and easily whether the book is worthwhile for our purposes. We hope that you, too, will find this checklist helpful in selecting nonfiction trade books for teaching content area subjects.

REFERENCES

Armbruster, B.B., & Anderson, T.H. (1981). *Content area textbooks* (Reading Education Rep. No. 23). Urbana, IL: University of Illinois Center for the Study of Reading.

Burke, E.M., & Glazer, S.M. (1994). *Using nonfiction in the classroom.* New York: Scholastic.

Irwin, J.W., & Davis, C.A. (1980). Assessing readability: The checklist approach. *Journal of Reading, 24*, 124–130.

Richards, P.O. (1994). Thirteen steps to becoming a children's literature expert. *The Reading Teacher, 48*, 90–93.

Vacca, R.T., & Vacca, J.L. (1993). *Content area reading* (4th ed.). New York: HarperCollins.

Creating and using a database of children's literature

Alice P. Wakefield

VOLUME 48, NUMBER 4, DECEMBER 1994/JANUARY 1995

Many teachers report that as they break away from the exclusive use of basal readers and start using more trade books in their classrooms, their students show signs of enjoying reading more. For these students, the authentic literary event of reading for pleasure during school hours is a more common occurrence than it used to be! Further, these students react as people everywhere do when they enjoy a good book; they tell someone about it. The student grapevine, which is usually confined to chatter about after-school events, now regularly includes frank comments about books and authors the students have read. The word gets around about books that should not be missed, as well as those to avoid.

If the above description sounds like what you have observed in your own classroom, it may be that your class would benefit from creating a database of children's literature. This project is natural for any classroom of readers. It combines the desire of one reader to document a good or not-so-good book with a modern, technological tool designed to assist other readers in their search for just the right book to enjoy.

Basically, a computer database program offers a way to organize information about books for easy retrieval. For example, readers would input pertinent data about books they have read by typing their responses to each of the data fields of the database. (See Figure 1.) A student looking for a good book to read may search the database to find a book of particular interest. Perhaps a student is interested in a specific subject. This subject can be found searching the database by using descriptors that have been used when entering the data. (See Figure 2.) Older elementary school children might find the genre category useful, as they search for another interesting mystery, science fiction story, or historical novel to enjoy.

As with most technology in the classroom, students rarely have any hesitation about trying it out. Most young readers are capable of learning to search the database for books to read for pleasure or for assigned research projects. As they read

Figure 1
Suggested fields for children's literature database

1. Title
2. Authorlast (Author's last name)
3. Authorfirst (Author's first name)
4. Illustlast (Illustrator's last name)
5. Illustfirst (Illustrator's first name)
6. Publisher
7. Copyright (year)
8. Grade for which selection is suitable (1, 2, 3, etc.)
9. Format (pop-up, picture book, photo, beginning reader)
10. Genre (folktale, nonfiction, mystery, poetry)
11. ThemeI (primary issue)
12. ThemeII (other possible issue)
13. ThemeIII (other possible issue)
14. Plot (three-sentence summary)
15. Awards (specify name and year of award)
16. Quality points (scale to be developed by class)
17. Reviewer (name of reader)

new books, students can continually add to the database.

Setting up the format of the database is not difficult even for the least experienced computer operator. Teachers who dare to try this project will be delighted with the results. Not only will the children's literature database be useful to them, but it will offer their students a powerful classroom tool that they can both use and contribute to by adding their own book reviews.

There are several database programs readily available for Apple (both the IIe and the Mac) and IBM-compatible computers. MECC (Minnesota Educational Computing Corporation) has a simple program for the Apple IIe computers called Book Worm. My first attempt was with the AppleWorks database on the Apple IIe with only 128K of computer memory. Presently, I am using dBase III + on an IBM-compatible computer. I have over 800 book reviews stored on my 1.3M high density diskette. The Mac can offer similar storage.

No matter what computer database program is available at your school, go find the program manual and get started. The suggested format guides in this article can be used as a model to create your own children's literature database. Your classroom environment will be all the richer for your efforts. Good luck!

Figure 2
Theme descriptors used in database of children's literature

Theme descriptor and what it includes

ABC . . . . alphabet books
Amphibians . . . . frogs, toads, salamanders
Animals . . . . all zoo, farm, extinct, bones, habitat, babies
Birds . . . . migration, nesting, birds of prey, eggs, feathers
Bugs . . . . butterflies, mosquitoes, metamorphosis, cocoon, crickets, spiders, ants
Career . . . . jobs, training, community helpers, tools
Characteristics . . . . brave, generous, kind, patient, responsible
Concepts . . . . colors, shapes, numbers
Cooking . . . . measuring, food
Environment . . . . recycle, pollution, ecology, ecosystem, conservation, food chain, littering
Family members . . . . siblings, stepparents, parents, grandparents
Family problems . . . . divorce, sibling rivalry, new baby, moving, death
Feelings . . . . self-esteem, prejudice, vanity, loneliness
Friendship . . . . getting along, cooperation
Garden . . . . vegetables, fruits, nuts, seeds (edible), harvest, soil, compost, tools
Health . . . . illness, death, disability, nutrition, risky behavior, medicine, intervention
House pets . . . . dogs, cats, hamsters
Money . . . . trade, making change, value, shopping, foreign
Multicultural . . . . customs, other cultures, foreign language
Ocean . . . . seashore, sea life, shells
Peace . . . . conflict resolution, war
Plants . . . . seeds, trees, leaves, moss
Pretend . . . . witches, ghosts, leprechauns, magic, unicorns, elves, trolls
Regions . . . . other countries
Reptiles . . . . snakes, turtles, lizards
Seasons . . . . winter, weather, holidays, rain, clothes, wind
Space . . . . travel, planets, stars
Sports . . . . recreation, competition, rules, losing/winning
Time . . . . telling time, past events, calendar, future
Transportation . . . . travel, vehicles, roads, maps, compass, direction
United States . . . . geography/history of states

On time and poetry

Joanne Durham

VOLUME 51, NUMBER 1, SEPTEMBER 1997

The Mouse whose name is Time
Is out of sound and sight.
He nibbles at the day
He nibbles at the night.

He nibbles at the summer
Till all of it is gone...

From "The Mouse Whose Name Is Time" from *Robert Francis: Collected Poems, 1936–1976* (Amherst, MA: University of Massachusetts Press, 1976). ©Copyright 1976 by Robert Francis.

The mouse called *Time* nibbles away all day long in my classroom. In cahoots with his buddies—the intercom, assemblies, snow days, and standardized tests—he chews up hours I planned for sustained reading, writing, responding, and understanding, leaving them punctured like Swiss cheese.

It is partly because of the constant presence of this mouse that I postponed seriously teaching poetry for my first 3 years of teaching elementary school. I have always loved reading and writing poetry, so I naturally wanted them to be a part of my classroom delights. But I teach in a school where 72% of the students qualify for free or reduced-price lunch and that has the dubious distinction of having the lowest state test scores in our county. Every moment of teaching time counts, and I needed to be clear about what would be accomplished by spending time on poetry. Every time I created a long list of objectives for teaching poetry I stopped myself. I refused to ruin poetry by teaching it.

Poetry every day

During my first 3 years I skirted the issue, doing isolated poetry events and lessons here and there. But this year, encouraged by a new team teaching arrangement, I decided to begin. I had come to understand the power in ritual—how a short, daily dose of an activity allows students to grow into learning, each at his or her own rate. From the first day of school I read a poem to my class at the end of the day. This was a time when we related things we each did that day that we were proud of, we talked about suggestions for making our class a better place, and I read aloud. A poem a day seemed like an appropriate part of this routine.

Shortly after I started the daily poetry reading, I put five or six poetry books and a decorated shoe box (the Poetry Request Box) on a shelf. Students completed small forms with their name, a book title, a poem title, and a page number. They checked whether they wanted to read it aloud or wanted me to read it aloud. Then they put the form in the box and I picked a few out each day and we shared those poems. The choice of reading aloud or having the poem read was done to encourage reluctant or shy readers, as well as more confident ones, to get involved with the poetry shelf. It also insured that I had ample opportunities, at the children's requests, to continue to read aloud and thus provide a model for the student readers.

My fourth-grade students were predominantly African American, with about one third of the class Latino or Asian. I chose anthologies of African American poetry including *Make a Joyful Sound* (Slier, 1991), *Pass It On* (Hudson, 1993), as well as the wonderful *A Caribbean Dozen* (Acard & Nichols, 1994), a collection of Caribbean poets. I included an anthology of contemporary American poetry, *A Jar of Tiny Stars* (Cullinan, 1996), a few books by specific poets, and rounded out the collection with some "type" books: *Noisy Poems* (Bennett, 1987), Mary O'Neill's (1961) color poems in *Hailstones and Halibut Bones*, Eloise Greenfield's (1988) poems written from paintings in *Under the Sunday Tree*.

The Poetry Request Box was an immediate hit with 8 to 10 girls in the class and a few boys. I worried that poetry would only appeal to girls and I was careful to select boys to read whenever they submitted requests. Some students submitted so many requests that we had to set a limit.

The procedure is simple. The student reads the poem including the author's name, shows the illustrations, and we clap. If there is information about the poet or the poet's views on writing in the book, we usually look for it and read it. If a student reads the poem too softly or haltingly for everyone to understand or fully appreciate, I praise the effort and reread the poem aloud. I emphasize how we often want to hear a poem a second time, to take it all in and enjoy it more. Sometimes I respond to the poem aloud; sometimes I encourage students to make pictures in their minds. If a poem has a particularly interesting rhyme or imagery, I ask students to listen for this or I point it out. Occasionally we use the "say something" process to share our reaction to the poem with a partner and then share some of these reactions with the whole group. Many times we simply listen and enjoy.

I found that when I picked the names and students immediately came up to read, many of them stumbled over words and didn't project well to the class, so I began picking the requests for the next day to give the children a day to prepare. They could practice before school, while waiting for bus call, at recess, or during free time. As a result the number of children who began to submit poetry requests significantly increased, especially among the less able readers. The opportunity to practice was vital to developing the confidence to get in front of the class and read. It also became a wonderful teaching time. I spent much of those same segments of the day coaching students individually to read their poems. We had conversations about words they don't understand, the meaning of the poem, facts about the poet, as well as strategies for sounding out words.

I have also learned better ways to coach them. At first, I listened to them read and helped them sound out words. Then I realized that hearing the poem read well the first time gave a struggling reader something to aim for and helped him or her to have a cohesive sense of the poem. Now I begin by reading the poem to a struggling reader. Then I ask what pictures the student saw in his or her mind, how the child feels about the poem, and we go back and sort out the meaning line by line. As we are doing so, the student becomes more engaged with the poem, brings in his or her prior knowledge, and uses meaning clues as well as phonics to remember difficult words.

It didn't take long before the wonderfully inevitable occurred: A student, inspired by our daily poetry readings, brought in the poem she had written at home and asked to share it at circle time. I was delighted as she shared her poem, and I made many positive comments, such as how well the ending worked. A few days later another student brought in a poem he had written, the ending of which was clearly influenced by the first child's, something else worthy of a big, positive fuss. From that day on, students have continued to bring in their own poems to share. Later in the year, one student, by her own initiative, created an anthology of poems written and illustrated by authors in our class. This book, which she titled *Take a Look*, proudly sits on the poetry shelf, and students write requests to read the poems of student poets in it.

Extending poetry

By early November, poetry was clearly playing a special role in our class, so I decided to expand it by holding a poetry festival. I grouped the students into heterogeneous groups; gave them a number of poetry books; had them choose a poem to perform; and had them decide how to make props, memorize, and present the poem on stage to an audience.

My students came to me with poor strategies for making meaning as they read. Even those who were fairly fluent tended not to focus on meaning, so I considered the most important thing I could do to help my students with reading was to teach them to read for meaning. My work with poetry led me to reflect on the relationship between reading poetry and developing comprehension. Poetry is probably the form of reading one can most appreciate without fully understanding the words. Poetry works on rhythm and sound as much as on word knowledge and meaning. In a way, that makes it safe and more enjoyable for struggling readers, gets them focused on reading, and provides the opportunity for making meaning. Furthermore, the short, compact form of the poem helps a student attempt to understand the meaning of a whole piece of writing without fragmenting it over time.

I have found that assigning students to prepare a poem for presentation helps them concentrate on comprehension. Students must think about what vocal expression is appropriate to the poem's meaning and which props bring the poem's most important aspects to the visual dimension. Even to decide where one voice should end and another should begin, a group needs to think together about which lines best belong to one idea. There is an added benefit for struggling readers. To memorize a poem, it must be read many times. By practicing over and over, struggling readers can sound just as fluent in the presentation as the more able readers. Their confidence is thus raised, and with their confidence, their enjoyment and willingness to take more risks in reading.

For about 2 weeks, the poetry festival dominated the day. I chose Gwendolyn Brooks's (1990) beautiful "A Little Girl's Poem" as the grand finale in which everyone had a part. We practiced the finale every day and used what we learned as a model for the small groups in their interpretations of their own poems. I also built a number of activities around the festival to further enhance reading, writing, art, math, thinking, and cooperative decision-making skills. In addition to the activities mentioned above, we wrote invitations, had an art contest for the cover of the written program, a speech writing and presenting contest for the emcee, did math lessons to figure out refreshments, tallied and graphed our favorite kinds of poems for decorations, and wrote program notes about the poets and poems. Clearly an authentic task, the festival motivated students to participate fully and eagerly in these various activities.

We invited several other classes, as well as parents and staff, to attend the program. It was the first time many students had performed on the auditorium stage with a speaking role. They experienced all the emotions attached to performance: nervousness, the fear of taking the risk to perform, and exhilaration and pride of accomplishment. The cooperative aspects of the festival, and particularly of the finale, became part of our shared experience. After the festival, one child remarked, "In the poem they had happy cocoa together. That was just like us. We came back to class after the poetry festival and had happy juice together." The concept of literary allusion was born in my fourth graders, not from lecture but from experience.

We continued soaking up learning from the poetry festival even after it was over. The students came back and wrote about the festival and illustrated and displayed their writing. We estimated how many people had come. I wrote a poem telling them how proud I was of their work.

Student involvement with poetry

After the poetry festival, we launched into writing workshops and publishing books, and many students chose to write poetry. The quality of their writing and how they went about it were considerably aided by the exposure they had already had to hearing poetry and presenting it themselves. We began to explore the way poets choose to divide their lines and develop an idea or image. Writing poetry became so prestigious in my classroom that I began to have problems with plagiarism. We discussed the difference between using a poet's work as inspiration or as a pattern to follow, and putting your own names on someone else's writing. One way I'm trying to solve this problem is by encouraging students to make anthologies of poems they like, illustrating them and/or adding editor's notes to them, but crediting the original poet.

Meanwhile, each day another child puts a poetry request in the box. I no longer have an imbalance between boys and girls. My most emotionally problematic child practiced and read and is impatient for his next turn. Most of my English for Speakers of Other Languages children have chosen to read. Students come back from the school library with poetry books. They eagerly tackle selections by Shakespeare and John Greenleaf Whittier; students delight in finding poems for special occasions, like Martin Luther King's birthday or our first snowfall. They dig out poems I didn't even know we had.

Poetry has become woven into our class rituals. For example, when our student teachers were leaving, I suggested students find poems to read on their last day. Four students, after pouring through our collection for the appropriate poem and searching more at home that evening, came up with poems so perfect they moved our student teachers to tears. Eloise Greenfield's (1988) poem, "To Friendship," which ends "...let's eat," be-

came a ritual to read before we shared special treats. My students understand there is a poem for every moment, feeling, and experience, and others waiting to be written by someone.

The incident that propelled me to write this article occurred after my teaching partner had discovered a live mouse in our classroom. A student who struggles to read found the poem, "A Mouse Whose Name Is Time," and immediately set about to share it with us in honor of the mouse. We spent several mornings, recesses, and afternoons together, all at his own initiative, and we discussed the poem's metaphor. He worked hard to conquer words like *seer* and *sibyl*, as well as more common ones that were beyond his vocabulary. Each morning he came in eager to apprise me of his progress. When he read aloud to the class, every student sat still through the entire poem, even though they couldn't hear a lot of it. They were "silent as a mouse" and clapped enthusiastically at the end while the student reader beamed. I recognized then how powerful poetry in my classroom had been and resolved to share it with other teachers.

Effects of daily poetry

I wanted poetry in my classroom for its affective power, its ability to inspire children to love language and, therefore, be more inclined to read. I have seen that happen and more. I have learned that sharing poetry as a daily ritual also affects the climate of the classroom. Poetry helps us to be aware of our feelings and to notice and appreciate our surroundings. Sharing those feelings and observations through poetry this year has helped humanize the interactions between children. Sometimes, as with the "happy juice" we drank together after the poetry festival, it has even given us the shared language with which to express and celebrate our interactions.

Poetry has also validated who my students are and has given them concrete examples of who they can become. They have learned about and read the works of poets of their own ethnicities and nationalities, as well as those of the European tradition. When someone chooses a poem from *A Caribbean Dozen* (Acard & Nichols, 1994), the students always ask to see the page about the poet. When we locate the place of the poet's origin, there is a murmur of satisfaction from the children from that country. They know that African American poets sometimes choose to write about universal subjects in standard English, and other times they choose themes related to their history and culture or write in Black English dialect. They know, by that exposure, that those unlimited choices await them as well.

If poetry had only served to motivate my students, I might still be conflicted as to poetry's role in my classroom. After all, my job is not only to inspire my students but to teach them the skills to meet the challenges of that inspiration. However, poetry has been successful on both the affective and cognitive levels. Heightening student interest in poetry has allowed me to better meet their immediate cognitive needs in developing reading, writing, and thinking skills.

Because my students have learned to expect a poem to connect with their daily lives, many have taken the risk to try writing their own ideas down on paper. They have experienced delight in the sound of words and the images those words make in their heads, and as a result, they have become more attentive to sounds and images. One day when a student was reading the description of a carnival in a novel he cried out, "Ms. Durham, this sounds like poetry!" Because they enjoy hearing poems read with expression, they are more eager to work on their own reading with expression. Students who have experienced the practice it takes to do a good job of reading a poem to the class, and have experienced the sense of success and accomplishment when they were done, are easier to convince to practice and to keep trying when confronted with other tasks. They want to understand, so they are learning to reread, make pictures in their minds, and connect with their own knowledge. These are the same habits and strategies they need to read a story, a science article, or the newspaper. All this has been accomplished based on about 10 minutes at the end of the day when a lot of "hard teaching" is unlikely to occur.

I believe I have struck a winning bargain with the Mouse Whose Name Is Time. He still nibbles mercilessly at my day, but neither fire drills, nor visitors, nor a thousand other interruptions consume our poetry time: It is sacred. The children have learned to grab other moments of the day for poetry on their own initiative. Hardly an indoor recess period goes by now in my class without a cluster of students at the poetry shelf. I have to chase them away from writing requests every morning when the bell rings and shoo them from the shelf to catch their buses in the afternoon. I know the Mouse has won a small victory when I can't let them spend more time on poetry, but I think about all the years of their lives after fourth grade. They are intrigued by poetry. They will find Time.

REFERENCES

Acard, J., & Nichols, G. (Eds.). (1994). *A Caribbean dozen: Poems from Caribbean poets*. Cambridge, MA: Candlewick Press.

Bennett, J. (Ed.). (1987). *Noisy poems*. Oxford, England: Oxford University Press.

Brooks, G. (1990). A little girl's poem. In P.B. Janeczko (Ed.), *The place my words are looking for* (pp. 60–61). New York: Macmillan.

Cullinan, B.E. (Ed.). (1996). *A jar of tiny stars: Poems by NCTE award-winning poets*. Honesdale, PA: Boyds Mills Press.

Francis, R. (1992). The mouse whose name is Time. In X.J. Kennedy & D.M. Kennedy (Eds.), *Talking like the rain* (p. 79). Boston, MA: Little, Brown.

Greenfield, E. (1988). *Under the Sunday tree*. New York: Harper Trophy.

Hudson, W. (Ed.). (1993). *Pass it on: African-American poetry for children*. New York: Scholastic.

O'Neill, M. (1961). *Hailstones and halibut bones*. New York: Delacorte.

Slier, D. (Ed.). (1991). *Make a joyful sound: Poems for children by African-American poets*. New York: Checkerboard Press.

Text sets: One way to flex your grouping—in first grade, too!

Michael F. Opitz

VOLUME 51, NUMBER 7, APRIL 1998

Grouping children to teach reading is one of the most prevalent practices in schools today. It's a good thing because grouping has several advantages. For example, it enables students to learn from one another as they discuss ideas found in various texts. As a result of listening to and discussing with others, students often gain new insights. Grouping also better ensures that all students will participate. Because groups are usually small, students get the opportunity to share their thoughts.

While grouping in general is advantageous, sole use of ability grouping—the grouping of children according to like overall reading achievement levels—is not. In fact, this type of grouping yields several unintended consequences especially for the children viewed as "low" readers (see Opitz, 1997, for a full review of these consequences). For example, students in the "low" group are often asked to perform low-level tasks and have fewer opportunities to read and write. These students' self-concepts are lowered, and they often feel excluded from the class.

Fortunately, there are alternatives, and the purpose of this article is to explain one—text sets. I have deliberately chosen to focus on first grade because this is when most children begin to see themselves as readers. How important it is, then, to have all children experience the reading of real books right from the start. And how fortunate for the children that authors, illustrators, and publishers have made many excellent titles available for them.

Text sets

What are they?

Text sets are collections of books related to a common element or topic. Single copies of books are often used to create them, with each student reading a different book related to the topic. See the Figure for six sample text sets appropriate for use in first grade.

Why use them?

One of the main reasons for using text sets is that they enable all children to be

Sample text sets

Alphabet

Grover, M. (1997). *The accidental zucchini*. San Diego, CA: Harcourt (Voyager). ISBN 0-15-201545-0.

McDonnell, F. (1997). *Flora McDonnell's A B C*. Cambridge, MA: Candlewick. ISBN 0-7636-0118-7.

Murphy, C. (1997). *Alphabet magic*. New York: Simon & Schuster. ISBN 0-689-81286-8.

Pomeroy, D. (1997). *Wildflower A B C*. San Diego, CA: Harcourt. ISBN 0-15-201-41-6.

Testa, F. (1997). *A long trip to Z*. San Diego, CA: Harcourt. ISBN 0-15-201610-4.

Animals

Duffy, D. (1996). *Forest tracks*. Honesdale, PA: Boyds Mills. ISBN 1-56397-434-7.

MacDonald, S. (1997). *Peck, slither, slide*. San Diego, CA: Harcourt. ISBN 0-15-200079-8.

Sturges, P. (1996). *What's that sound, wooly bear?* Boston: Little, Brown. ISBN 0-316-82021-0.

Threadgall, C. (1996). *Animal families*. New York: Crown. ISBN 0-517-88548-4.

Counting

Bohdal, S. (1997). *1, 2, 3 What do you see?* New York: North-South. ISBN 1-55858-646-6.

Cousins, L. (1997). *Count with Maisy*. Cambridge, MA: Candlewick. ISBN 0-7636-0156-X.

Sierra, J. (1997). *Counting crocodiles*. San Diego, CA: Harcourt. ISBN 0-15-200192-1.

Tucker, S. (1996). *1, 2, 3 Count with me*. New York: Simon & Schuster. ISBN 0-689-80828-3.

Gardening

Cole, H. (1995). *Jack's garden*. New York: Greenwillow. ISBN 0-688-13501-3.

Florian, D. (1991). *Vegetable garden*. San Diego, CA: Harcourt. ISBN 0-15-201018-1.

Ford, M. (1995). *Sunflower*. New York: Greenwillow. ISBN 0-688-13301-0.

Lobel, A. (1990). *Alison's zinnia*. New York: Greenwillow. ISBN 0-688-08865-1.

Peterson, C. (1996). *Harvest year*. Honesdale, PA: Boyds Mills. ISBN 1-56397-571-8.

Relationships

Bogacki, T. (1997). *I hate you! I like you!* New York: Farrar, Straus, Giroux. ISBN 0-374-33544-3.

Fox, M. (1997). *Whoever you are*. San Diego, CA: Harcourt. ISBN 0-15-200787-3.

Kroll, V. (1997). *Hands*. Honesdale, PA: Boyds Mills. ISBN 1-56397-051-1.

Neitzel, S. (1997). *We're making breakfast for mother*. New York: Greenwillow. ISBN 0-688-14575-2.

Yolen, J. (1997). *Nocturne*. San Diego, CA: Harcourt. ISBN 0-15-201458-6.

Shapes

Dodds, D. (1994). *The shape of things*. Cambridge, MA: Candlewick. ISBN 1-56402-224-2.

Falwell, C. (1992). *Shape space*. New York: Clarion. ISBN 0-395-61305.

Grover, M. (1996). *Circles and squares everywhere!* San Diego, CA: Harcourt. ISBN 0-15-200091-7.

MacDonald, S. (1994). *Sea shapes*. San Diego, CA: Harcourt. ISBN 0-15-200027-5.

Merriam, E. (1995). *The hole story*. New York: Simon & Schuster. ISBN 0-671-88353-4.

exposed to "real" books right from the start. The result? Children see themselves as readers.

Moreover, using text sets enables children of different achievement levels to be grouped together to learn about a given topic, thereby warding off the stereotyping and other negative consequences of ability grouping.

Not only do text sets allow for heterogeneous groups, but they also permit the limited resources to be spread further. That is, because only one copy of each book is needed, a variety of books can be purchased rather than multiple copies of a single text.

How are they used?

Text sets are used during guided reading instruction. Once students are grouped, the teacher provides each student with one of the books and conducts the reading lesson. As with any effective guided reading lesson, the teacher provides guidance before, during, and after the reading.

Here's a sample framework:

Before reading

1. Activate background knowledge.

"Today we're going to read some books about gardening. What can you tell me about gardening?" As students share their ideas, they are written on the chalkboard or on a chart for future reference.

2. Set the purposes for reading.

"I have a book for each of you to read. When I give you your book, read the title and take a picture walk through the book. Be ready to tell the rest of us what you think your book will be about." Students are given a few minutes to complete this activity.

During reading

1. Explain to students what they will be doing.

"Now that you've had a chance to look through your book, please read it silently to see if you are right about your book. I'll be here to help you if you need it."

2. Have students read silently to see if their predictions were correct. Provide help as needed.

Note: Because some of the books will take longer to read, students could be provided with some additional activities if they finish reading before others in the group. Writing in a journal, drawing about their favorite part of the book, or reading another book are all viable activities.

After reading

1. Plan time for students to tell about their books. Also ask students what their books have in common. A comparison/contrast lesson in which students tell and list how their books are alike is a natural.

2. Complete additional follow-up activities as desired. Students could read a favorite part of their books or show a picture that they liked the best.

Getting ready

Thinking through the logistics of text sets before students arrive will better ensure their success and yours, too. Here are five suggested steps:

1. Identify the topic you want your students to explore. Ask students what they would like to learn more about.

2. Identify your students' general achievement levels. This can be done by using a set of graded passages or specific books that have been identified as "benchmark books."

3. Locate books with varying reading difficulty levels related to the topic. When determining levels, consider interest, levels of predictability (see Peterson, 1991), as well as appropriateness for your specific students and grade level.

4. Determine how many students you want to have in the group. I have found four or five to be ideal. Make sure that you have a "just right" book for each student—books that correspond to their overall achievement levels.

5. Organize your students into groups so that you can read with one group while the rest are completing other activities.

Concluding thoughts

As you attempt using the text sets shown here or those you create, remember that feeling comfortable with this way of teaching may take some time. This is true with almost any teaching strategy that is new to the repertoire. Take time to celebrate successes along the way.

REFERENCES

Opitz, M. (1997). *Flexible grouping in reading: Practical ways to help all students become better readers*. New York: Scholastic.

Peterson, B. (1991). Selecting books for beginning readers and children's literature suitable for young readers. In D.E. DeFord, C.A. Lyons, & G.S. Pinnell (Eds.), *Bridges to literacy: Learning from Reading Recovery* (pp. 119–147). Portsmouth, NH: Heinemann.

Come alive stories

Elizabeth J. Dewey

VOLUME 48, NUMBER 4, DECEMBER 1994/JANUARY 1995

A beautiful girl in a long, gold satin ballgown walked down the hall with a royal, hairy beast for a companion. Is this real or imaginary? For a moment, the children wonder. Are they really at school? This was the beginning of a most extraordinary day.

As a first-grade reading teacher, I wanted to organize a schoolwide event to promote oral and written language. Storytelling had all the elements I wanted. Listening to, talking about, and telling stories fire students' imaginations, build oral communication skills, and establish language experiences to draw on later. What a perfect student-centered activity to promote reading new stories and writing stories of their own! I had to bring storytelling to our school!

The San Antonio Storytellers association helped me locate tellers who could tell stories to young children. Our parent-teacher organization approved funds for the tellers, purchased certificates and commemorative pencils for each child, and provided a luncheon for the storytellers and faculty to become acquainted. Spurred by this support, I asked our high school theater arts teacher if high school

drama students, in costume, could present short skits from well known children's stories. She and her students spent several weeks preparing scripts and elaborate costumes for *Beauty and the Beast*, *Aladdin and Jasmine*, *The Princess and the Pea*, and *Cinderella*.

My goal in organizing the festival day was for each child to experience a variety of storytellers in both small- and large-group settings. Therefore, storytellers visited individual classrooms during the morning so they could tell their tales to small groups of eager listeners. In the afternoon, two 45-minute storytelling concerts took place in a large meeting room where several classes of students could attend together. Each concert featured three storytellers.

Finally, on a sunny morning in May, our elementary students began a most extraordinary school day, like no other all year. The tools of learning were not books, pencils, or chalkboards. Instead, children used their senses, their feelings, and their imaginations as they became part of our storytelling festival. They listened intently as the storytellers wove visions of places, characters, and situations into a tapestry of wonderment. Colorful words drifted through every classroom and filled every corner. At the end of this magical day, each child left with a storytelling certificate and a plethora of images to encourage retellings at home.

The happenings, now a vivid memory for the children, marked a beginning for their teachers. Ideas took shape as teachers spoke with each other and discussed ways to incorporate storytelling into their own classroom activities.

One perceptive teacher saw the advantage of using storytelling to stimulate talk and writing. She said, "If a teacher were a storyteller, she could teach anything. How can I learn storytelling?"

Another teacher suggested that the children could interview a grandparent (or other family member) and write a family history story. The finger-string pictures one storyteller had used interested another class, and they wanted to learn more about this art form. Their teacher decided to pursue this interesting method for teaching sequencing and following directions.

One writing connection that the children made naturally happened during lunchtime. Our eight happy, costumed, high school students paid an unscheduled visit to the school cafeteria. The teenage celebrities were as excited as the children! They walked among the tables, shaking hands with the wide-eyed youngsters.

"Don't forget to eat your peas. Aladdin loves peas!" one teenager said enthusiastically.

"Hi! I'm Cinderella. I love your dress. Do you like mine?" "Sure, you may touch it!"

Instinctively, wanting to preserve this moment forever, a little boy picked up an unused napkin and said, "Aladdin, can I have your autograph?"

Authors are a big deal

Ally McArdle
Mary Buchholz

VOLUME 47, NUMBER 2, OCTOBER 1993

Celebrate authors and children's literature by creating an Authors' Card Game of your very own. Commercially available card games feature classic authors, but students know which authors they enjoy reading. Creating the game is easy.

We began by brainstorming the names of popular authors with the class. We were amazed at the long list of authors the class compiled. From that list, each pair of students chose an author and listed four of his or her books. For some pairs, this meant a trip to the card catalog in the library or research in various books about authors and their works. We kept a list of partners' names and authors chosen so the class set would contain no duplications.

After the students had investigated their author and his or her works, they drew rough drafts of their cards, listing the titles in rotating order and drawing sketches to correspond with each featured title.

The accompanying diagram shows a set of four rough-drafted cards for one author.

After completing and correcting the rough drafts, students put the same information on 4"×6" index cards (10×15 cm). Each student completed two cards (10×15 cm). Each student completed two cards, and each pair of students had a complete set or "book" for each author.

The cards were then copied onto colored construction paper, stamped on the back so sets would be easy to identify, and laminated. The sets were cut apart and returned to the students. Our game included cards representing 12 authors. Students can play the game according to the rules outlined below which are similar to "Go Fish," or can make up their own rules.

Students learned about the author they researched, and in playing the game, they also discovered new and exciting authors. Celebrating authors and children's literature was a pleasure with the Authors' Card Game.

Rules for Authors' Card Game

The object of the game is to complete "books" or sets of four cards from each author. The cards are shuffled and each player is dealt four cards, one at at time. The remaining cards are placed in a pile, face down, in the center of the table. To start, the player at the dealer's left asks for a specific book title from a specific player. If the player has that title on the top of a card, it is given to the caller. The caller continues to ask for titles until he or she fails to receive the requested title. Then a card is drawn from the pile by the caller. The next player to the left gets a turn, and so on. When a player gets a complete book of four cards by one author, it is set aside. After all the cards have been gathered into books, the player with the most books wins.

Sample rough draft of a four-card set for books by Chris Van Allsburg. The children print a different book title at the top of each card. A simple illustration for that book is drawn in the box. Below the author's name, the students print the remaining three titles for that author.

Author birthday celebration

Lauren J. Behar

Volume 49, Number 1, September 1995

Last August I was visiting one of my favorite book stores. Totally engrossed with the excitement of children's literature surrounding me, I noticed a bulletin board highlighting children's authors born in August with some book jackets displaying their literature. My first thought was, "What a great idea!" But, then again, this was a book store. What other birthdays would be displayed? Then my thoughts drifted back to my classroom and the birthday board. Including authors' birthdays with children's birthdays for each month would be a wonderful way to relate to an author and his/her work, by personalizing it for the children. I received a list of authors born each month of the year from the bookstore. This became my guide.

The bulletin board display now consists of paper balloons with the names of the children and their birthdates. Also included are paper book jackets with the names and dates of authors born in that month. I reproduce a character from one of the author's books and place it on the board as well (see Figure 1).

At the beginning of each month, children born in that month are given an Author-Birthday Presentation sheet (see

Figure 1
Birthday bulletin board

Figure 2). They choose an author born in their birthday month from those displayed on the bulletin board. Then they locate information about the author and write a

---

Figure 2
Author—birthday presentation

---

1. Choose an author born in your birthday month.
2. Collect information about your author.
   - birthdate
   - first book
   - birth place
   - childhood
   - other interesting facts
3. Write a short report using the information gathered.
4. Read at least two books by the author.
5. Choose a creative way to present your author's work.
   Examples: character mobile
                 diorama
                 puppet show
                 picture TV
                 other ideas!!
6. Present report orally to the class.

---

brief summary. In addition, they read two books by their author and create a project related to one of the books read.

At the end of the month, the children choose a day to present their author project orally to the class. On that day, the student's presentation is shared, and PQP (Praise, Question, Polish) statements are offered from peers. Then the student celebrates his/her own birthday with refreshments.

The children's responses to this activity are evident in their excitement as they anticipate who the authors will be that share their birthdays. Their creative projects are enthusiastically presented. Dioramas, games, and puppet theaters are just a few of the wide range of projects presented. One child created a newspaper from the time of Laura Ingalls Wilder, which included biographical information.

At the end of the year, it is thrilling to discover the number of authors with whom the children are familiar and the associations they can make with their work. We commonly hear statements like, "Have you read Chris Van Allsburg's new book?" Authors have become personal friends.

More predictable books: Gateways to a lifetime of reading

Marianne C. Saccardi

VOLUME 49, NUMBER 8, MAY 1996

In this article I overview some of the latest predictable books for emergent readers that develop a sense of rhythm and entice children to play with words, and I make suggestions for using these books in the classroom.

Developing a sense of rhythm

Young children respond to and learn about life through their bodies. They love to touch, to taste, to see, to hear, to move. It is not enough for us to explain to them what rough and smooth mean. They need to touch rough and smooth objects. It is not enough for us to talk about sand. Children must see it, pour it, build with it, and discover what it feels like. If we want beginning readers and writers to be able to control language, then they must also experience language in their bodies, feel its rhythms and movements. Predictable books enable children to do this.

In Helen E. Buckley's *Grandfather and I* (1994) and its companion book *Grandmother and I* (1994), a young child contrasts leisurely activities with his grandparents and the hectic nature of life with parents and siblings:

> Grandfather and I
> never hurry.
> We walk along
> and walk along
> and stop...
> and look...
> just as long as we like.
> Other people we know
> are always in a hurry.
> Mothers hurry.
> They walk in a hurry
> and talk in a hurry.
> And they always want **you** to hurry.

Text of poem "Grandfather and I" from *Grandfather and I* by Helen E. Buckley. Copyright ©1994 by Helen E. Buckley. Reprinted by permission of Lothrop, Lee & Shepard Books, a division of William Morrow and Company, Inc.

Print these words on a chart or overhead transparency and invite the children to read and clap. They will notice that their hands and voices move faster in the section about mothers than in the section about grandfather. Meaning is conveyed as much by the rhythm of the chosen words as by the words themselves. This is important information for budding writers to store for a time when they will have sufficient control of language to use it themselves.

Children can also clap to the rhyming couplets in Katie Evans's *Hunky Dory Found It* (1994), a simple story about a dog that finds and collects objects dropped by his family or neighbors. Have individual children clap each page while the entire class claps the refrain, "Hunky Dory found it."

Preston is a young pig without a care in the world. In Colin McNaughton's funny book *Suddenly!* (1994), he goes on an errand for his mother, never realizing that on numerous occasions he narrowly escapes being eaten by a wolf. Just as the wolf is about to pounce, something "suddenly" happens to change Preston's location. Young readers, of course, are aware of Preston's danger. But they are in for a bit of a surprise at the end as well. Bring out the rhythm instruments and have the children make booming sounds to accompany the word "suddenly" each time it appears in the story. This will give them a sense of how that one word, boldly written, can interrupt the action.

Of course, the best way to give children a sense of rhythm in language is to surround them with poetry. Poetry can be highly predictable and easily read. Have poems on charts around the room. Take poetry breaks throughout the day. Clap poems, chant poems, put poems to music. Encourage the children to write their own poems as well. Douglas Florian's *Bing Bang Boing* (1994), Fay Robinson's *A Frog Inside My Hat* (1993), Virginia Tashjian's *Juba This and Juba That* (1995), and Nadine Westcott's *Never Take a Pig to Lunch* (1994) are just a few of the many fine new poetry books available for use as predictable books.

Playing with words

Because words are the writer's tools (Fletcher, 1993), we need to give young readers and writers many opportunities to experiment and play with them. Make classroom lists or charts of favorite words encountered in stories, or encourage children to keep their own lists. Celebrate the times children use words well in their writing or speaking. Choose a variety of predictable books that are rich sources of well-crafted writing.

What Would You Do If You Lived at the Zoo? (1994) by Nancy White Carlstrom is a playful book in question-and-answer format with cutout shapes through which children may peek at the zoo animals. The answers are filled with nonsense words: "I would waddle with the pig... kapoodle kapuddle kapong!" There are also wonderful verbs such as *prowl, prance, shuffle, romp, chomp, waddle, cuddle,* and *strut.* Once children become familiar with this book, they can read it antiphonally, half of the class asking the questions and the other half answering. They can write additional animals into the story, making up their own nonsense words and finding new verbs to go with them.

While less predictable than many of the other books discussed here, Jonathan London's *Like Butter on Pancakes* (1995) does have some rhyme and repetitive elements and is especially enjoyable for its beautiful language. This is a story in which "slippers whisper" and "First light melts like butter on pancakes, spreads warm and yellow across your pillow."

Write the text on charts or overhead transparencies. As you read it aloud several times, have children visualize the scene and copy their favorite words or phrases. Transfer these to strips and distribute several strips to different groups of children. Give the children time to arrange the strips in any way that sounds pleasing to them. The results can be pretty amazing.

While not new, Paul Geraghty's *Over the Steamy Swamp* (1989) has recently been issued in paperback by Harcourt Voyager and may be more available to classrooms. A food chain develops when a hungry mosquito flies over a swamp and each creature views the one it is watching as a potential meal. The language in this wonderful book is as lush as the steamy swamp itself: "famished frog," "peckish fish," "stealthily slithering snake," "craving crocodile," "hostile hunter," "hysterical heron" and so many more. Point out the alliteration. Discuss strategies for figuring out what the words mean. Set up an art gallery of creatures drawn by the students with two-word descriptive captions beneath each picture.

In Erica Silverman's *Don't Fidget a Feather* (1994), a gander and a duck have a contest to determine which one is the true champion of the world. They agree that the one who remains perfectly still without "fidgeting a feather" the longest is the winner. Both animals remain firm against trying odds, even when a fox prepares to eat them for dinner. In the surprise ending, readers learn about the stuff of true greatness. After hearing the story several times, the children might enjoy working in groups to write and illustrate their own alliterative phrases, for example, "don't attack an ant" or "don't bury a banana."

Conclusion

Accomplished readers build on a body of knowledge they acquire over time. They constantly compare information in different books and interact with the text to make meaning, identify with characters, solve problems, and shed light on their own lives. It is a joy-filled journey without an end. Beginning readers are on the first leg of that journey, and predictable books can help them along the way. The books we choose and the literacy tasks in which we are engaged with our students can introduce them to the wonders of a lifetime of reading and learning.

REFERENCE

Fletcher, R. (1993). *What a writer needs.* Portsmouth, NH: Heinemann.

CHILDREN'S BOOKS CITED

Buckley, H.E. (1994). *Grandfather and I*. New York: Lothrop.

Buckley, H.E. (1994). *Grandmother and I*. New York: Lothrop.

Carlstrom, N.W. (1994). *What would you do if you lived at the zoo?* Boston: Little, Brown.

Evans, K. (1994). *Hunky dory found it*. New York: Dutton.

Florian, D. (1994). *Bing bang boing*. San Diego, CA: Harcourt Brace.

Geraghty, P. (1989). *Over the steamy swamp*. San Diego, CA: Harcourt Brace.

London, J. (1995). *Like butter on pancakes*. New York: Viking.

McNaughton, C. (1994). *Suddenly!* San Diego, CA: Harcourt Brace.

Robinson, F. (1993). *A frog inside my hat*. New York: Bridgewater.

Silverman, E. (1994). *Don't fidget a feather*. New York: Macmillan.

Tashjian, V. (1995). *Juba this and juba that*. Boston: Little, Brown.

Westcott, N.B. (1994). *Never take a pig to lunch*. New York: Orchard.

Cultural diversity + supportive text = Perfect books for beginning readers

Michael F. Opitz

VOLUME 52, NUMBER 8, MAY 1999

The 1990s brought several new picture books that reflect our increasingly diverse society. How fortunate for the children we teach! Indeed, few would dispute that all children need books that represent their cultural heritage. In this way all children have characters with whom they can identify. As Galda (1998) notes, "All readers...need books that allow them glimpses of the selves they are, visions of the selves they'd like to become, and images of others that allow them to see beyond who they are" (p. 275). These books also provide children with opportunities to learn about similarities and differences among people and to consider different points of view. In the end, many of these books help to create a sense of community among children by showing them that despite differing cultural backgrounds, there are commonalities among us all.

Beginning readers also need books that facilitate successful independent reading experiences. Books such as these are predictable books because they are written with specific language features (i.e., supportive text) that help the reader to predict words and events in the story. Pictures also support the text, providing additional help. From the very beginning, children see themselves as readers of "real" books.

Using books such as these helps to develop independent lifelong readers. This development happens in the following manner: Because the text is supportive, the novice reader can read it with ease. Reading with ease enables the reader to enjoy the experience and feel successful and confident. Consequently, the reader chooses to repeat the experience. Meaningful practice occurs during the repeated readings and provides the reader with opportunities to develop fluency and other important reading skills such as comprehension and vocabulary. An expanded repertoire of skills permits the reader to read increasingly complex material.

This article provides an annotated bibliography of books that address cultural diversity while providing supportive text simultaneously. All of the books in this bibliography were published in the 1990s and were selected using the following criteria:

- The book needed to celebrate diversity or show common bonds among all people in some way. Some of the books such as *Play* (Morris, 1998) contain pictures that represent people from many different cultures engaging in similar activities. Others, such as *Tortillas and Lullabies/Tortillas y cancioncitas* (Reiser, 1998), address a specific cultural group.

- The text needed to offer support to beginning readers via the language features that the author used to create the text. Language features such as rhyme, rhythm, repetitive sentences or phrases, cumulative text, and familiar sequences and events support beginning readers as do books containing pictures that reinforce the text. The Figure provides an overview of these books and the language feature(s) each offers. The Figure also shows the books that feature both Spanish and English. Books are listed alphabetically by title.

- All of the books needed to be authentic texts—texts written to communicate ideas rather than to use specific high-frequency words a given number of times throughout the text. Authentic texts come in varying levels of difficulty and are illustrated in many different styles.

- While reading aloud has many benefits, children must independently read texts to become proficient readers. Therefore, the annotated books listed here are meant to be read by novice readers rather than to them. True, an appropriate book introduction to ensure successful reading is still necessary. However, introducing books is beyond the scope of this article. Interested readers may want to read an article written by Marie Clay (1991) that provides a detailed explanation and a wealth of suggestions for book introductions geared toward individual needs.

- The books needed to be appropriate for youngsters. The vocabulary and story lines needed to be suitable for beginning readers in kindergarten or first grade.

Happy reading!

Annotated bibliography

Code: *Title, Year, Author, Illustrator, Publisher (location and name), ISBN, Annotation.*

Action alphabet. 1996. Shelly Rotner (author and photographer). New York: Atheneum. 0-689-80086-X.

This book shows children from a variety of cultural groups completing actions common to many children—climbing, diving, and eating to name a few. Each page features one word that names the picture.

America: My land, your land, our land. 1997. W. Nikola-Lisa. Illustrated by 14 American artists. New York: Lee & Low. 1-880000-37-7.

Through rhyme and illustrations that depict many cultural groups, readers experience the many characteristics of the United States. Pictures of the illustrators are accompanied by explanations of their pictures and a brief biography.

Supportive book characteristics

Title	Date published	Rhyme/rhythm	Repetition	Cumulative text	Familiar events/sequence	Supportive pictures	Spanish & English
Action alphabet	1996				✔	✔	
America: My land, your land, our land	1997	✔	✔			✔	
Coconut Mon	1995		✔		✔	✔	
Cumbayah	1998	✔	✔			✔	
Feast for 10	1993	✔	✔		✔	✔	
Fiesta!	1996		✔		✔	✔	✔
Greetings, Sun	1998	✔	✔		✔	✔	
Hands!	1997		✔		✔	✔	
I am me!	1996				✔	✔	
My five senses	1998		✔		✔	✔	
Navajo ABC	1995				✔	✔	
No mirrors in my Nana's house	1998	✔	✔			✔	
Now I'm big	1996		✔		✔	✔	
Play	1998				✔	✔	
Somewhere today	1998		✔		✔	✔	
Tortillas and lullabies	1998		✔		✔	✔	✔
Uno, dos, tres; One, two, three	1996	✔	✔		✔	✔	✔
When I first came to this land	1998	✔	✔	✔		✔	
Whoever you are	1997		✔			✔	
Whose hat?	1997		✔			✔	
Work	1998				✔	✔	

Coconut Mon. 1995. Linda Milstein. Cheryl Taylor. New York: Tambourine. 0-688-12862-9.

A Caribbean coconut man sells 10 coconuts, one at a time.

Cumbayah. 1998. Floyd Cooper (illustrator). New York: Morrow Junior Books. 0-688-13544-7.

Cooper provides a verse of this familiar song on each two-page spread. Different cultural groups are used to illustrate each verse. The musical score is provided on the inside front and back covers.

Feast for 10. 1993. Cathryn Falwell (author and illustrator). New York: Scholastic. 0-590-48466-4.

A family works together to prepare a feast—from shopping to the actual feast. Ten steps are used to shop, and 10 are used to prepare the feast.

Fiesta! 1996. Ginger Foglesong Guy. Rene Moreno. New York: Greenwillow. 0-688-14331-8.

Several children collect a variety of items for a party, although the purpose isn't discovered until the end of the book. In addition to receiving opportunities for predicting how the collected items might be used, readers are also provided practice in reading and counting to 10 in Spanish and English.

Greetings, Sun. 1998. Phillis Gershator and David Gershator. Synthia Saint James. New York: DK. 0-7894-2482-7.

Two children greet the sun and nearly every other object they see throughout a day—from the time they arise until the time they go to bed.

Hands! 1997. Virginia Kroll. Cathryn Falwell. Honesdale, PA: Boyds Mills. 1-56397-051-1.

Hands can be used in many ways as this book well illustrates. The text emphasizes that joining hands with others is one of the most meaningful ways to use hands.

I am me! 1996. Alexa Brandenberg (author and illustrator). San Diego, CA: Harcourt Brace. 0-15-200974-4.

This book shows children imaging themselves in their future careers as well as activities they will do in the meantime.

My five senses. 1998. Margaret Miller (author and photographer). New York: Aladdin Paperbacks. 0-689-82009-7.

Children explore their five senses and discover how they help in everyday life.

Navajo ABC: A diné alphabet. 1995. Luci Tapahonso and Eleanor Schick. New York: Simon & Schuster. 0-689-80316-8.

This book presents one object valued by the Navajo Indians for each letter of the alphabet. A glossary provides additional information about each word.

No mirrors in my nana's house. 1998. Ysaye Barnwell. Synthia Saint James. San Diego, CA: Harcourt. 0-115-201825-5.

A young girl tells how she found out about herself even though her nana's house had no mirrors—she looked into her nana's eyes. The text is both spoken and sung on the CD that accompanies the book.

Now I'm big. 1996. Margaret Miller (author and photographer). New York: Greenwillow. 0-688-14077-7.

Several children talk about activities they did as babies as well as what they do now that they are older and bigger.

Play. 1998. Ann Morris. Ken Heyman, photographer. New York: Lothrop. 0-688-14552-3.

People from all over the world engage in play in this book. An index that tells more about each picture is provided as is a map that encourages the reader to connect each picture with the country where it was taken.

Somewhere today. 1998. Shelley Moore Thomas. Eric Futran, photographer. Morton Grove, IL: Albert Whitman. 0-8075-7545-3.

This book shows ways that people can do things to help others and create peace along the way.

Tortillas and lullabies/Tortillas y cancioncitas. 1998. Lynn Reiser. Corazones Valientes. New York: Greenwillow. 0-688-14628-7.

A young girl tells about family customs by explaining activities that her great-grandmother and grandmother did for their daughters—activities that she does for her doll. The text is written in both English and Spanish.

Uno, dos, tres; One, two three. 1996. Pat Mora. Barbara Lavallee. New York: Clarion. 0-395-67294-5.

Two girls go from store to store to buy birthday presents for their mother. Readers are provided with opportunities to read the numbers one through 10 in Spanish and English. A pronunciation guide is provided at the end of the book.

When I first came to this land. 1998. Retold by Harriet Ziefert. Simms Taback. New York: Putnam. 0-399-23044-0.

A traditional song is used to describe the adventures of a pioneer who comes to America, buys a farm, and builds a brand-new life for himself and his family. A map of the United States and territories in 1885 is shown in the front and back covers.

Whoever you are. 1997. Mem Fox. Leslie Staub. San Diego, CA: Harcourt. 0-15-200787-3.

The commonalities of all children are emphasized throughout this story. Although we may look different, Fox shows how we are alike through our feelings and actions. "Whoever they are, wherever they are, all over the world" is the refrain that repeats throughout the book.

Whose hat? 1997. Margaret Miller (author and photographer). New York: Mulberry Paperback. 0-688-15279-1.

Many hats are worn by people who complete many different types of jobs. This book invites readers to guess who wears the various kinds of hats featured throughout.

Work. 1998. Ann Morris. Photographs provided by many photographers. New York: Lothrop. 0-688-14866-2.

People from all over the world are engaged in work in this book. An index that tells more about each picture is provided along with a map to connect the reader with the country in which it was taken.

REFERENCES

Clay, M. (1991). Introducing a new storybook to young readers. *The Reading Teacher, 45,* 264–273.

Galda, L. (1998). An annotated bibliography of multicultural children's literature. In M. Opitz (Ed.), *Literacy instruction for culturally and linguistically diverse students* (pp. 275–277). Newark, DE: International Reading Association.

Exploring bias using multicultural literature for children

Jim Barta
Martha Crouthers Grindler

VOLUME 50, NUMBER 3, NOVEMBER 1996

Multicultural education provides an opportunity for young students to examine the diversity shaping our world. Through such efforts, students learn about variations of culture, such as the ways people speak, act, celebrate, or mourn. Students learn, for example, that although we all speak to communicate, different languages or dialects are used. We all wear clothes, but the style and pattern of our clothing varies greatly. The message is that people do similar things in different ways. If children learn of our similarities, this awareness may overshadow the fear of differences.

The use of children's literature can serve as a significant tool in helping expose children to the ways others express their culture. Multicultural literature focuses on people of color, regional cultures, religious minorities, the disabled, or the aged or describes female perspectives or issues (Harris, 1992). It reflects multiple perspectives of culturally diverse authors. Numerous multicultural books that receive high praise are published yearly and add to the increasing list of those that already grace our shelves. These books allow us to explore lands far and near with story characters who may seem very unlike ourselves. Examination of cultural diversity takes place when students discuss people different from themselves involved in situations in which they may have had no direct experience.

But is the examination of differences enough? Cultural differences are not always perceived positively, particularly when viewed from the perspective of the mainstream culture. Simply reading about cultural variations may do little to affect the degree of inequality in our society. If cultural variations were viewed as merely different ways that people do the same things, all variations would be valued equally. however, it is the negatively biased responses to these variations that lead to discriminatory behavior. Bias against diversity, not diversity itself, is the cause of the turmoil.

Bias leading to prejudice and discrimination is so prevalent in some societies that many people are nearly blind to its existence. When a negative bias blends so completely into the patterns of daily life that it is no longer perceived or challenged, it becomes institutionalized. Creating an awareness of a negative bias towards others is the goal toward which we should educate. If used thoughtfully, children's multicultural literature can help us reach this goal.

Multicultural literature can serve a number of purposes (Campbell & Wittenberg, 1980):

1. It heightens respect for individuals. Children discover that all people have basic needs, feelings, and emotions.

2. It acknowledges contributions of minorities. Many cultures have made contributions to the world, and we should celebrate these accomplishments.

3. It brings children into contact with other cultures. Since children develop an awareness of differences among people at an early age, it is important that they be exposed to books that reflect a pluralistic society. This helps to eliminate ethnocentrism and encourages respect and tolerance for others.

4. It enhances students' self-concept. Children realize that they have a cultural heritage of which they can be proud.

5. It helps children realize that society has developed a value system that validates some differences and minimizes others. This system is based on ignorance and misperception and its existence promotes inequality.

6. It encourages students to detect prejudice and to work toward its elimination.

Educators must guide their students in critical analyses of what they read in order to achieve these purposes. Multicultural literature provides opportunities to learn more about others and to examine societal or individual responses to the cultural context. The Figure suggests a procedure for exploring bias in children's multicultural literature.

To illustrate the bias exploration procedure, the children's book *Flossie and the Fox* (McKissack, 1986) will be used. The procedure begins with children reading or listening to this story (Phase 1) of a young girl who has been asked by her mother to carry a basket of eggs to her aunt's house. On the way, she meets a fox intent on getting those eggs. This wonderful story describes Flossie's conversation with the fox as she confounds it with her composure and cleverness. Often this book is read to enjoy the story of Flossie outwitting the fox and to experience an African American dialect. The book is enjoyed, the eggs and Flossie are safe, and "dat olde fox's fumin." This book, however, can provide for extensive study of cultural variation.

Phase 2 suggests that teachers identify with their students the cultural aspects of the character(s) that are different from those of the mainstream. In this book, Flossie speaks English but in a way that differs from mainstream American English speakers. To explore bias and extend the learning, students could identify, list,

Exploring bias in children's literature

Phase 1: Reading multicultural literature

Phase 2: Defining cultural variation(s)

Phase 3: Discussing the mainstream response(s) to the variation(s)

Phase 4: Describing the common behavior represented by the variation

Phase 5: Exploring the error of the negatively biased responses and offering students unbiased information concerning the variation and its cultural context

or chart ways in which Flossie uses her African American country dialect to express her thoughts and feelings. Specific words or phrases could be listed and their meanings rewritten into the mainstream language of the classroom.

Phase 3 has teachers and students discussing the ways that some individuals, or society in general, may perceive, evaluate, and respond negatively to these differences. Flossie's language reflects her culture, her heritage, and her experience. This style of dialect is often referred to as Black English Vernacular and has been perceived by some as the incorrect way the poor or the uneducated speak. At this point, the teacher may ask his or her students if they consider a French, an Irish, or a Swedish person speaking English with

an accent (or using nonstandard English) to be poor or uneducated. Generally, these variations are not seen in the same light as that of the African American dialect speaker. European English dialect may instead be perceived as cute or quaint, but seldom is it negatively regarded. This perceptual incongruence reflects the existence of bias, and it is at Phase 3 that the exploration and discussion of bias begin.

During Phase 4, students describe the behavior(s) common to all people represented by the variation. When variations are viewed through an unbiased perspective, it is discovered that all people share specific common behaviors. The point in this analysis is that although all people use words to communicate, language is specific to the context. Humans, as multilingual communicators, switch "codes" to meet the demands and the expectations of the situation. We speak to very young children differently than we do to our teachers or our employers. Certainly there is a necessity to competently use standard American English to succeed in U.S. society, but other dialects following culturally appropriate, sophisticated, and systematic grammatical conventions need not be minimized in order to do so. Helped to learn this important fact, children will soon realize the wonder of verbal diversity as negative bias is explored.

Phase 5 encourages the further study of the variation. Through this exploration, students are able to see firsthand how negative bias develops through ignorance and is disarmed when accurate information concerning the cultural variation is shared. For example, comprehensive study of African American country dialect teaches students that the language evolved from a number of African languages and incorporates a consistent and rule-bound grammatical system. In every sense of the word, it is a correct language that has been misperceived by those who do not fully understand its history or significance (Dandy, 1991). When this learning is shared, students grow to validate the language and, therefore, the culture of speakers of this dialect. As knowledge is gained, negative bias is diminished.

Some educators and parents may argue that children are simply too young to be exposed to issues of bias, prejudice, and discrimination. The more suitable argument should be why have educators and parents allowed the travesty of prejudice against people of color, the disabled, the aged, and women to persist for so long?

Unless we begin to adapt our curriculum to explore negative bias, the solution to this problem will exist just beyond our reach. We may soothe our consciences by addressing these societal problems when we include multicultural literature in our instruction, but until we take the next step by exploring prejudice to the cultural variations shared, we do little more than support its existence and participate in its perpetuation.

REFERENCES

Campbell, P., & Wittenberg, J. (1980). How books influence children: What the research shows. *Interracial Books for Children Bulletin, 11*(6), 3–6.

Dandy, E. (1991). *Black communications: Breaking down the barriers*. Chicago: African American Images.

Harris, V. (1992). Multiethnic children's literature. In K.D. Wood & A. Moss (Eds.), *Exploring literature in the classroom: Content and methods* (pp. 169–201). Norwood, MA: Christopher-Gordon.

McKissack, P. (1986). *Flossie and the fox*. New York: Dial.

"Monstruos," "pesadillas," and other frights: A thematic unit

Carol Evans

VOLUME 47, NUMBER 5, FEBRUARY 1994

I recently sat in a cozy library kiva with first-grade bilingual children listening to scary stories. It was 2 days before Halloween, and anticipation was high. The librarian delighted the children by animatedly telling and reading stories in English and Spanish. Most of the children were dominant in Spanish, but they understood English as well, as shown by their comments in Spanish. The end of each story was punctuated with excited chatter and laughter from the children about their own reactions to these little tales.

For some time, I have been fascinated by children's interest in scary stories. This recent experience, as well as some new reflections on the potential usefulness of such stories in elementary school literacy programs, has inspired me to organize the bilingual literacy unit described here. This unit is organized primarily for children through the third grade, who, by studying and discussing scary stories, may learn more about this body of literature and thereby also discover ways of coping with fear themselves.

A universal human phenomenon, fear has been the inspiration for a large and time-honored body of adult literature. And clearly, the tales in this unit can readily become stepping stones in building more sophisticated literary interests and tastes for the likes of Edgar Allan Poe's stories, Henry James's novellas, and a great deal of science fiction, to give a few examples. But perhaps more importantly, these tales for children may intimately illustrate that most basic utility of literary works—the power to provide a mirror in which personal experience can be examined and reflected upon. In this case, the experience is that of being frightened; the reflections can center on the sources of fear, the ways in which human beings can help each other in frightening circumstances, and some of the ways in which fear can be overcome.

The experience of fear, especially the irrational fears of nightmares and imagined events, is universal, but the cultural forms of its literary expression vary. This has two implications. First, since important cultural differences exist in the types

42

of scary stories typically told to or written for children, teachers must reflect on their own culturally shaped tendencies to accept some types of stories while excluding others that may be quite appropriate and developmentally useful for children in their teaching communities. Given the need to incorporate not only children's home language but also their family (and therefore their cultural) experiences as valued and legitimate sources of school study and learning (McCarty, Lynch, Wallace, & Benally, 1991; Moll & Diaz, 1987), the unit should include examples of traditional tales or *leyendas* which, as part of the living literature of the community, may be quite salient for the children. The second implication is that in viewing tales from different cultures, children may recognize cultural perceptions at variance from their own. In examining these differences in a classroom that is itself culturally respectful and responsive, children may develop insights about themselves and about their own culture or cultures.

A bilingual literary unit

Hudelson and Rigg (1992) described bilingual literary units organized around parallel themes as portrayed in carefully selected Spanish and English texts. If properly implemented, this arrangement in a Spanish/English bilingual classroom assures that all children will find literary enrichment in their first language while developing increasing capacity in their second.

This unit about fear derives from the same basic concept and principles. The texts listed may prove useful in discussion of fear; however, they are only suggestive of the variety of possibilities. Children will be able to read many of the tales, but others may be more successfully read aloud by the teacher. In addition to the literary exposure and the thematic understanding that are a part of the unit, children may learn about types of scary tales, recognize distinguishing literary elements and language, create new storybooks or plays of their own, an develop related vocabulary through their reading and writing.

The unit may be conceptualized in a number of ways, but teachers may want to focus on developing children's understanding in two main areas: the origins of fear and ways of overcoming it. In the first place, children will better understand both the fears of the protagonists in the stories and their own fears if they are helped to distinguish between two universal types of fear. The key difference between the two types is where the fear begins: (a) outside us—fears of being harmed by a real of imagined person, animal, or other powerful figure or force; or (b) inside us—fears in which our own anxieties cause us to imagine or project frightening objects or forms.

The first type of fear arises from the sense of helplessness and danger that we feel from time to time in the presence of persons, animals, or forces that seem to threaten to overpower or harm us. They inspire fear because we know that in some form they do in fact exist. *La Llorona* is a traditional tale well known to most Mexican Americans in which a mother mourns for her two drowned children. She bears the responsibility for their drowning, and inconsolably distraught, she returns from the dead hoping to recover them. She wanders in desperation in the darkness, ready to snatch even innocent children who come into her view. The menace of the wandering ghost notwithstanding, this tale is terrifying because of its verisimilitude. Most of us have felt mothers' fears for their children, and we can easily imagine that the mother in this story would be desparate and might never rest. Many of the other traditional tales also concern this type of fear.

In quite a different story, *Turquesita*, which is not frightening but is about fear, a small young fish who wishes to swim through a narrow passage to a feeding area favored by many fellow fish is frightened by the strong currents at the entrance to the passage. She has swum near the entrance and felt the currents, and her experience with them inspires fear. Turquesita consults with several adults about the actual strength of the currents and, once reassured, swims through determinedly of her own volition. (See Cribbet-Bell, 1989; Perales, 1972; Sauvageau, 1975; and Uribe, 1984 for other examples of fear whose source lies outside us.)

The other type of fear begins with the anxieties inside each of us, anxieties we generally learn to keep well under control. On occasions when these inner worries overpower us, as in our dreams, our imaginations may project creatures or forces that threaten to harm us. Thus we manufacture the monsters of nightmares and the dreadful beings of dark rooms and cemetaries. Nan Bunilda, protrayed as a child dwarf fairy in *Comienza la aventura*, delights in conquering imagined foes in daily play but is terrorized by more powerful monsters in her nightmares.

The boy in *Harry and the Terrible Whatzit*, perhaps becasue he feels small and vulnerable, imagines that something terrible resides in the dark and musty basement of his house. Yet fearing for his mother's welfare, he descends in to the basement and bravely confronts the two-headed monster of his fears. (See Company, 1985b; Crowe, 1976; Galdone, 1982; Mayer, 1987; and Viorst, 1973 for other examples of fear whose sources lie inside us.)

Overcoming fear is accomplished in two general ways in these stories: (a) people help each other, or (b) children learn to cope with fear themselves. The stories of *Harry and the Terrible Whatzit* and *Turquesita* illustrate both. Harry overcomes his dread of the basement and Turquesita her fear of the currents. But each is aided in the process by a friend or family member who seems to understand the fear and is supportive and encouraging. This sort of help is also illustrated in *My Mama Says There Aren't Any Zombies, Ghosts, Vampires, Creatures, Demons, Monsters, Fiends, Goblins, or Things*, in which the mother cuddles a child who imagines monsters lurking everywhere.

Similarly, Nana Bunilda, the dwarf fairy with the nightmares in *Comienza la aventura*, is helped by her parents who let her jump in their bed when she has wakened from a nightmare. Later her grandmother helps with both information and advice, ex-

Sample bilingual texts

Cribbet-Bell, C. (Ed.). (1989). *Tales told in our barrio: A Carrillo Intermediate Magnet School Project.* Tucson, AZ: Carrillo Intermediate Magnet School, Tucson Unified School District. A collection of brief tales from a school community.

Hayes, J. (1987). *La llorona: The weeping woman.* El Paso, TX: Cinco Puntos Press. Traditional legend of the Southwest.

Sauvageau, J. (1975). *Stories that must not die.* Austin, TX: Publishing Services, Inc. A collection of traditional tales in four volumes. Parallel texts in English and Spanish in a side-by-side format.

Sample texts in Spanish

Company, M. (1985a). *Comienza la aventura.* Madrid: Ediciones EM. A girl who plays fearlessly in the daytime, but suffers from nightmares when she goes to sleep, learns to handle the monsters in her dreams.

Company, M. (1985b). *Nana Bunilda come pesadillas.* Madrid: Ediciones EM. Nana uses her special flying machine to zoom to the rescue of children having nightmares.

Dubovoy, S. (1991). *Turquesita.* Mexico: Edicion D.R., Consejo Nacional para la Cultura y las Artes. A young fish is afraid of the strong current but learns to trust her own power in confronting it.

Gutierrez, D., & Oliver, M.F. (1987). *La noche de estrellas.* Caracas, Venezuela: Ediciones Ekare-Banco del Libro. A shepard finds his work difficult because he's afraid of the dark.

Perales, A.M. (1972). *La lechuza: Cuentos de mi barrio.* San Antonio, TX: Naylor Co. Traditional legends of the Southwest.

Uribe, V. (Ed.). (1984). *Cuentos de espantos y aparecidos: Coedicion latinoamericana.* Sao Paolo, Brazil: Editora Atica: Legends of Latin America.

Sample texts in English

Crowe, R. (1976). *Clyde Monster.* New York: Dutton. A monster learns not to be afraid of the dark.

Gackenbach, D. (1977). *Harry and the terrible whatzit.* New York: Scholastic. A boy overcomes his fear of the basement when he goes looking for his mother and confronts the "monster" there. Also available in Spanish.

Galdone, P. (1982). *The monster and the tailor: A ghost story.* New York: Clarion. The Grand Duke commands his tailor to sew at night in the cemetary. The tailor is frightened by the appearance of a monster but escapes unharmed.

Mayer, M. (1987). *There's a nightmare in my closet.* New York: Dial. A child imagines a nightmare in his closet.

Viorst, J. (1973). *My mama says there aren't any zombies, ghosts, vampires, creatures, demons, monsters, fiends, goblins, or things.* New York: Aladdin. A child imagines monsters everywhere; his mother denies it but comforts him in the end.

plaining that the monsters are a function of Nana's own imagination and encouraging Nana to take charge, not to let her imagination have control. Nana uses her grandmother's advice and learns to cope with her nightmares herself. Years later, as a grownup in *Nana Bunilda come pesadillas*, Nana offers support herself, flying to the rescue of children suffering from nightmares. (The books in the Figure by Company, 1985a, 1985b; Crowe, 1976; Dubovoy, 1991; Gackenbach, 1977; Galdone, 1982; Gutierrez & Oliver, 1987; and Viorst, 1973 should be most helpful in discussions of overcoming fears.)

As unit-related activities, teachers may have children make lists of scary words or types of scary monsters. Children may draw their own monsters and create scary tales about them. They might, for instance, enjoy writing stories, adopting the format of the Viorst or Mayer texts. Children can interview parents and family members and create a collection of scary tales from the community. Parents or other storytellers from the community may be invited to the classroom. Following discussions of stories in which characters overcome their fears, children may enjoy creating other solutions for dealing with specific difficulties like fears of the dark or nightmares. With a bit of help, they may prepare a play to perform for other classes in the school or collect and illustrate a set of fear-reducing strategies for the classroom library. Finally, they might create a new story in which one of the characters they've read about overcomes some newly encountered frightening experience.

The author wishes to thank Edward Joseph Shoben, Jr. for his interest in this project and for his help in improving the author's understanding of the types of fear illustrated in these stories.

REFERENCES

Hudelson, S., & Rigg, P. (1992, March). *Multicultural literacy: Spanish and English books connecting the young and old.* Paper presented at the meeting of the Arizona Teachers of English to Speakers of Other Languages, Casa Grande, AZ.

McCarty, T.L., Lynch, R.H., Wallace, S., & Benally, A. (1991). Classroom inquiry and Navajo learning styles: A call for reassessment. *Anthropology and Education Quarterly, 22,* 42–59.

Moll, L.C., & Diaz, R. (1987). Teaching writing as communication: The use of ethnographic findings in classroom pratice. In D. Bloome (Ed.), *Literacy and schooling* (pp. 193–221). Norwood, NJ: Ablex.

Defining the "multi-" in "multicultural" through children's literature

Lara L. Hillard

Volume 48, Number 8, May 1995

Multicultural literature can introduce children to unfamiliar practices and concepts inherent to different cultures. In selecting multicultural literature, however, it is important to realize that culture is not exclusively a result of ethnic background. Many other factors, such as religion and geographical region, are also involved. Some teachers may select literature representing only one or two cultural groups to include in their classroom studies and think that they are promoting cultural diversity. To develop a truly multicultural curriculum, it is necessary to choose a wide variety of literary selections to represent many different groups. In order to do this, teachers must understand what multicultural literature is, why it should be used, and how it should be selected.

Definitions

What does multicultural mean as it pertains to literature? Ginny Kruse (1992) defines multicultural literature rather narrowly as "books by and about people of color" (p. 30). This definition does not take into account the wide spectrum of cultural differences that are independent of skin color. Many classroom teachers, however, seem content to use this definition as the sole basis for their curriculum.

Sleeter and Grant (1988) give a somewhat expanded definition for multicultural literature. They consider it to be the body of materials that "recognize, accept, and affirm human differences and similarities related to gender, race, handicap, and class" (p. 137). This definition still neglects cultural differences related to such factors as religion and geographical region.

In a much more inclusive definition of the term, Elizabeth Martinez views multicultural literature as that which "emphasizes respect for the different historical perspectives and cultures in human society" (Madigan, 1993, p. 169). This is a good definition because it leaves room to consider all facets of cultural diversity when selecting materials for classroom use. Teachers, as well as students, must come to realize that culture involves far more than that which can be seen on the surface.

Rationales

Once teachers understand what multicultural literature is, they need to determine a rationale for including it in the curriculum. One reason often given is that children learn more from situations with which they are familiar. The argument is that in the U.S., children who are not part of the Euro-American culture have been discriminated against in the public school curriculum. This may be a valid criticism, but in a class of 20 children, it will be difficult to find literature that reflects the background and experiences (i.e., culture) of each student.

Arlene Barry (1990) provides a more practical justification for a multicultural curriculum. She asserts that although we need to teach children that people are different, it is more important to point out the ways in which they are similar. Through these realizations, our students may acquire a sense of acceptance and appreciation for others. Children and adults need to understand that, regardless of cultural differences, we are all people with feelings, hopes, and dreams. If we teach children to acknowledge and understand these basic similarities, the differences will become much easier to accept and appreciate.

Materials

A third issue to be faced in the development of a multicultural curriculum is the selection of quality materials. One very important point is that the books chosen should meet the criteria for good children's literature regardless of content. Quality Euro-American literature should be used in conjunction with the excellent multicultural literature that is now available (Reimer, 1992).

Authenticity is a vital aspect of literature selection. The literature should contain an accurate portrayal of the culture presented. Characters and situations need to be representative and authentic. Educators must evaluate the details in both the illustrations and the text to verify that they give a true picture of the values and beliefs of the culture (Yokota, 1993). Using literature that gives inaccurate information can be more harmful than the failure to represent other cultures at all.

A third area to be considered is that of "hypersensitivity" (Reimer, 1992, p. 19). We must not get so caught up in being politically correct that we lose all sense of perspective. For example, some have argued over the inclusion of *Huckleberry Finn* because of the use of the term "nigger." Although it is unacceptable in today's society, Twain uses the term in a historically accurate portrayal of the early Southern U.S. culture.

We must realize the difference between being stereotypical and including cultural traits to avoid what Reimer (1992) terms a "watering down" (p. 19) of the curriculum, in which we include only literature that gives a positive portrayal of every aspect of the cultures with which it deals.

Conclusion

Every day we come into contact with individuals from a myriad of cultural backgrounds. The way we handle these encounters will be based largely on knowledge and attitudes derived from past experiences. The inclusion of quality multicultural literature is an excellent way to give children positive experiences that foster an acceptance and appreciation for cultural differences. To better prepare our students for the diversity found in our world, we must develop a curriculum that focuses on the inclusion and acceptance of all cultures rather than the selection and promotion of a few.

REFERENCES

Barry, A. (1990). Teaching reading in a multicultural framework. *Reading Horizons, 31,* 39–47.

Kruse, G. (1992). No single season: Multicultural literature for all children. *Wilson Library Bulletin, 66,* 30–33, 122.

Madigan, D. (1993). The politics of multicultural literature for children and adolescents: Combining perspectives and conversations. *Language Arts, 70,* 168–176.

Reimer, K. (1992). Multiethnic literature: Holding fast to dreams. *Language Arts, 69,* 14–20.

Sleeter, C., & Grant, C. (1988). *Making choices for multicultural education:Five approaches to race, class and gender.* Columbus, OH: Merrill.

Yokota, J. (1993). Issues in selecting multicultural children's literature. *Language Arts, 70,* 156–166.

Internationalism in Danish children's literature

Mary E. Blake
W. Gale Breedlove

VOLUME 47, NUMBER 3, NOVEMBER 1993

A very special benefit to everyone interested in international literacy is the ability to use literature to acquire information about others, especially those from different cultures, and to share information about themselves. Literacy and literature provide the much-needed bridges to world understanding and peace. The possibilities for exploiting links between literature and international awareness are many, especially if we start with the newest and youngest initiates to literacy, our children. One country which has done just that is Denmark, one of the most literate of the western countries (Blake, 1984), which incorporates international awareness and understanding within its varied, diverse, and multifaceted approach to literature for children and young people.

Literature and internationalism—The Danes' historical perspective

The idea of literature being linked to internationalism is not new for the Danes.

As far back as the time of Hans Christian Andersen (1805-75), Danish literature has been exported to other countries. As a writer and spinner of tales, Andersen traveled a great deal, and with his travels came the popularization of his work throughout Europe and the Western world. The very first English translation of his fairy tales was published in 1846. While Andersen's work is truly world literature, his tales are flavored with the ideas and the atmosphere of Northern Europe. He always wanted to be remembered as a Dane; the balanced, accepting tone of much of his work is typical of his Danish heritage (Bredsdorff, 1976). Through his fairy tales he allowed the rest of the world to become acquainted with that view—the good, the evil, the happy, the sad, and the bittersweet that are all part of life.

In more recent times, Danes have continued to benefit from the link between literature and international understanding. During the 1960s and 70s a series of seminars sponsored by the Danish National Commission for UNESCO explored the use of children's literature as a means of promoting intercultural understanding. The result of these seminars was a series of proposals for action based on the use of children's literature to portray honestly the multitude of cultures in the world. The Commission's belief was that these actions would lead to the promotion of intercultural understanding (Danish National Commission for UNESCO, 1977).

At the present time there is still a strong link in Denmark between literature and internationalism. Although this link is not always a conscious effort on the part of Danish educators, writers, publishers, or librarians, it does manage to take three discernible forms. First, a certain amount of Danish literature is exported and translated into other languages, giving readers in other countries a taste of Danish life and values. Additionally, certain Danish authors are interested in other cultures and have authentically used those cultures within their own Danish writings. Finally, because Denmark is a small language area (approximately 5 million people speak Danish), it becomes necessary for much literature to be imported and translated into Danish. These translations give the Danish young people a view of other cultures. Indeed, what we see in Denmark are some coincidental practices linking literature with an international view of the world.

Exported literature from Andersen to modern times

It is one thing to begin to appreciate other cultures through literature, but quite another to be able to export literature for others to appreciate. The Danes have accomplished both in times past and present.

Although accomplished in many forms of writing, Denmark's Hans Christian Andersen is known around the world for his fairy tales, written for grown-ups as well as children. Who can forget "The Emperor's New Clothes" in which the silliness of the adults is revealed by the child who tells what he sees—that the Emperor has no clothes, or "The Little Match Seller" who uses up her matches to keep alive the vision of her dead Grannie who comes to take her home with her? And in these days of equality and tolerance, the sad "Little Mermaid" who gives up everything to win the love of a mortal takes on new meaning, as does "The Ugly Duckling" who turns into the beautiful swan, assuming his rightful place in the world. What is remarkable is that all these tales echo Andersen's calm, balanced Danish view of the world.

Modern day Denmark has also produced magnificent storytellers, chief among whom is Bjarne Reuter. His most popular work is *Buster's World (Busters Verden)*, the 1990 winner of the Mildred L. Batchelder Award for best translated children's book in the U.S. Buster, the hero of the tale and a grandson of a circus performer, has problems both at home and in school. However, through his knowledge of circus magic, he is able to change his life—to make it humorous and hopeful.

For other readers, those bordering between young adult and adult, film and video have highlighted at least one other Danish author. In recent years Martin Andersen Nexo's *Pelle the Conqueror* has been filmed and acclaimed as an international success. It has now made its way to video stores, providing another way to acquaint those of other cultures with Danish literature. Andersen Nexo's story of Pelle,

the young boy and farm worker who dreams of leaving home and conquering the world, provides a sensitive human portrait as well as a picture of a social system in need of reform.

Danish authors and internationalism

Perhaps it is the Danes' basic attitude of respect for all life and tolerence for human differences that has been the most significant factor in Denmark's efforts to use children's literature to heighten awareness of other cultures and foster true internationalism.

Several Danish authors have produced works that present other cultures in an authentic manner (Schiff & Thorup, 1990). Many of these books relate information about life in countries where there are economic and social problems and concerns about freedom. Places such as Africa, Asia, and South and Central America are explored.

Central America is the setting for a number of books, including Kare Bluitgen's (1989) *Jaguaren Ved Verdens Ende* ('The Jaguar at the End of the World'). This story describes the world of a banana plantation and the conflict between the owner and his son, who disagree about how the plantation should be run.

Otto S. Svend provides a picture of the life of the children of the River Yangtze in *Bornene ved Yangtze Kiang* ('Children of the Yangtze River') (1982). This book includes a description of an actual flood that occurred in 1981. It is de-

---

Children's literature

Exported Danish literature

Andersen, H.C. (translated by Patricia Crampton). (1985). *Fairytales.* Copenhagen, Denmark: Carlsen.

Andersen, H.C. (translated by R.P. Keigwin). (1976). *80 fairy tales.* Odense, Denmark: Skandinavisk Bogforlag and Flenstad Forlag.

Andersen, Nexo, M. (1989, 1991). *Pelle the conqueror*, vols 1 and 2 (translated by Steven Murray and Tiina Nunnally). Seattle, WA: Fjord Press.

Reuter, B. (1980). *Busters verden.* Copenhagen, Denmark: Branner og Korch. *Buster's World*, Translated by Anthea Bell. New York: Dutton, 1989.

Danish internationalism

Bluitgen, K. (1989). *Jaguaren ved verdens ende.* Odense, Denmark: Gyldendal.

Bluitgen, K. (1988). *Bomuldens dronning.* Odense, Denmark: Gyldendal.

Bodker, C. (1971). *Dimma Gole.* Copenhagen, Denmark: Branner og Korch.

Bodker, C. (1970). *Leoparden.* Copenhagen, Denmark: Branner og Korch. *The Leopard* (translated by Gunnar Poulsen). New York: Atheneum, 1975.

Hoff, M. (1987). *Ojne der ser.* Odense, Denmark: Gyldendal.

Hultberg, U. (1982). *Der falder et trae.* Copenhagen, Denmark: Carlsen.

Svend, O.S. (1982). *Bornene ved Yangtze Kiang.* Copenhagen, Denmark: Glydendal. *Children of the Yangtze River.* Englewood Cliffs, NJ: Salem Press, 1982.

---

scribed through the eyes of the children who courageoulsy helped their elders in battling it. In 1978 Otto S. Svend won the international H.C. Andersen Award for his excellent work as an illustrator.

Cecil Bodker is a Dane who lived for some time in Ethiopia. She writes about that country in *Dimma Gole* (1971) and *Leoparden* ('The Leopard') (1970). In the first book Dimma Gole meets some Europeans and learns practices that he believes will help his own society. *Leoparden* describes the life of Tibeso, a shepherd, and the dangers that face him in a society riddled with social problems and suspicion.

Africa has also been the setting for books for by Mogens Hoff, *Ojne der Ser* ('Eyes which See') (1987); Ulf Hultberg, *Der Falder et Trae* ('A Tree is Falling') (1982); and Kare Bluitgen, *Bomuldens Dronning* ('The Queen of Cotton') (1988). Hoff's book describes the problems and joys of a Danish family's stay in Africa. *Der Falder et Trae* is the documentary of a village in Nigeria that is spoiled by the building of a motorway, and *Bomuldens Dronning* describes the ordeal of a girl and her family during student demonstrations in the South African town of Soweto.

These books and authors are but a sampling of what is available for young Danish readers. Other authors who have shown understanding of different cultures are Eva Asmussen, Aage Brandt, and Kjeld Koplev.

The Danes are not alone

Although the Danes are doing a commendable job in promoting a sense of internationalism in the world, they are not alone. Many world organizations and individual countries mirror their efforts.

The ability to appreciate, respect, communicate with, and learn from others around the world is a recurring theme of professional and service organizations in recent years (Breedlove, 1990). Leaders throughout the world have come to realize that international understanding must be embraced not only for world literacy but also for the survival of the species.

The authors wish to recognize Danes Ingelise Schiff of the Vedbaek School and Lise Thorup, a trained school library consultant, for providing necessary and valuable information on Danish authors. Their collaboration and support are greatly appreciated.

REFERENCES

Blake, M. (1984). Reading in Denmak: A relaxed attitude is the key. *The Reading Teacher, 38*, 42–47.

Bredsdorff, E. (1976). Introduction. In H.C. Andersen, *80 fairy tales* (p. 10). Odense, Denmark: Skandinavisk Bogforlag and Flensteds Forlag.

Breedlove, W.G. (1990). *Contemporary trends in children's and young adults' literature: Research perspectives.* South Carolina State Council of the International Reading Association.

Danish National Commission of UNESCO. (1977). *Children's literature as a means of promoting intercultural understanding* (Reporting of the international seminar in Denmark, 8/29–9/2/77). Copenhagen, Denmark: UNESCO.

Schiff, I., & Thorup, L. (1990). Personal communication.

Introducing art history through children's literature

Rita Greco

VOLUME 50, NUMBER 4, DECEMBER 1996/JANUARY 1997

Whole language has opened the gates for introducing a broader range of reading materials. Elementary reading programs have entered the world of traditional literature, history, science, mathematics, and the arts. The interrelationship of disciplines brought about by whole language inspires the teacher to seek new subjects to introduce to his or her class. Modern children's literature offers a diverse selection of interesting and appropriate material in the area of art history for the young reader.

Art history is a valid and exciting way to instill in children a love of both art and literature. Children are naturally attracted to art. When introduced to books about art and artists they often become consumed by what they learn and continue to seek more information on the subject. Through art history, a teacher will share with his or her class a visual history magnificently revealed through the beauty of painting and sculpture. The art will surprise and delight both the teacher and the class while their appreciation and understanding of it grow.

An extensive knowledge of art history and children's art is helpful; however, it is not essential because the teacher's goal is to instill an enjoyment of art through literature (and vice versa) rather than undertake a complete understanding of it. This is an area where the teacher and children can grow together in their appreciation of the arts. In addition, this growth can be enhanced when followed up with literature and projects concerning the children's own artistic endeavors. The school's art specialist may be helpful in suggesting activities to complement an art/literature program. In addition, there are many books that deal with such activities. Naturally, art activities make art history more relevant for the children.

There are two art history book series I found particularly enjoyable for children: *Art for Children* by Ernest Raboff (1988) and *Getting to Know the World's Greatest Artists* by Mike Venezia (1990). *Art for Children* is a series of books that presents the lives and works of the world's most recognized artists. Each book contains a short biographical sketch and helpful interpretations of the artist's works. *Getting to Know the World's Greatest Artists* is a series written for younger readers. It introduces five great artists and their artwork in a fun, whimsical fashion. In addition to the variety of books available for the young reader, there are an increasing number of audio and visual tapes, videos, and filmstrips on the market. Many schools also have a collection of art prints. The larger size of these prints enhances the children's appreciation of them.

Art and literature are natural companions. Bringing them together for the children to enjoy is a venture that should not be ignored.

REFERENCES

Raboff, E. (1988). *Art for children series*. Garden City, NY: Harper & Row.

Venezia, M. (1990). *Getting to know the world's greatest artists series*. Chicago: Children's Press.

Activities from a tall tales unit

Jaynie Nesmith

VOLUME 48, NUMBER 1, SEPTEMBER 1994

S ally Ann Thunder Ann Whirlwind Crockett, bride of Davey, is a little known tall tale character. Introducing Mrs. Crockett to a classroom of young children can be a wonderful entrée to the world of tall tales. With a beehive bonnet, a snake belt, and a dress of pelts, Sally Ann Thunder Ann Whirlwind Crockett accomplishes feats of wonder (Cohen, 1985). From stomping a litter of wildcats to battering Mike Fink, Sally Ann Thunder Ann Whirlwind Crockett exemplifies the old adage, "Behind every great man there is a great woman."

With the revival of storytelling in the United States, tall tales are becoming more popular with young children. Picture books by well-recognized authors and illustrators such as Steven Kellogg retell lively stories of such memorable characters as Paul Bunyan, Johnny Appleseed, and Pecos Bill. This is an opportunity to share a part of America's history in an engaging, enjoyable manner. The different occupations and the geographic locations mix reality and fantasy to stimulate the imagination. Whether dressing up in Sally Ann's picturesque outfit or reading a big book about Johnny Appleseed, children are captivated by the exploits of these legendary characters.

A tall tales theme lends itself well to all content areas and numerous activities. The following are just a sampling of the possibilities. They are written to the student so that they can be put on task cards to be included in a learning center or used in shared reading or writing activities. Reference books are included for each activity that might need information on the tall tales characters.

Language arts

1. Check how many of the tall tale characters are female. Feature these characters in a special "women of accomplishment" magazine article (Cohen, 1985; Dewey, 1988; Osborne, 1991; Purdy, 1985).

2. Make a chart of characteristics comparing super heroes and tall tale characters. Be sure to list likenesses as well as differences (Osborne, 1991; Zorn, 1992).

3. Working with a partner, describe an invention for Farmer McBroom's Almanac. An illustration can be included (Fleischman, 1984).

Social studies

1. After researching the tall tale characters, make a birthday tree and place their birthdates on it. For fictional tall tale characters you may find out when their first story was written (Osborne, 1991; Zorn, 1992).

2. Survey the teachers in your school for their favorite tall tale. Survey the children. Compare your results and publish your findings.

3. Plot the tall tale characters' home-sites on a map. Compare the number that lived in the west to those living in the east (Osborne, 1991).

Science

1. After reading about John Henry compare real pieces of steel, aluminum, and iron. How are they alike? Different? Write a description of each (Keats, 1965; Osborne, 1991).

2. Investigate how wolves, coyotes, and dogs are alike and different. How might the life of Pecos Bill have been different if he had been raised with wolves or dogs instead of coyotes (Gleeson, 1988; Kellogg, 1986)?

3. Research tornadoes. Compile a fact sheet. Compare the facts to the tornado in the story of Pecos Bill (Gleeson, 1988; Kellogg, 1986).

Math

1. Compare your height with that of Pecos Bill's bear. Find the difference (Gleeson, 1988; Kellogg, 1986).

2. Check the *Guinness Book of World Records* for the tallest man ever reported. Compare to Stormalong, Joe Magarac, Paul Bunyan, and John Henry (Osborne, 1991; Zorn, 1992).

3. Convert Stormalong's shoe size to metrics (Osborne, 1991).

Block activities

1. How many blocks would it take to build a chair for Paul Bunyan (Osborne, 1991)?

2. Build a wagon that rolls for Pecos Bill (Kellogg, 1986).

3. Build a house for Pecos Bill and Slue Foot Sue. How many different types of blocks did you use (Gleeson, 1988; Kellogg, 1986)?

Creative movement/ dramatics

1. Take Paul Bunyan steps. Swim a Stormalong lap. Lift a barbell as if you were Joe Magarac. Throw a Pecos Bill lasso. Ride a horse like Slue Foot Sue. Hammer as if you were John Henry. Shoot a gun like Davey Crockett. Run after Lightning (Kellogg, 1986; Osborne, 1991; Zorn, 1992).

2. Make up several rain dances (Gleeson, 1988; Kellogg, 1986).

3. Play charades acting out the tall tale characters (Osborne, 1991; Zorn, 1992).

Art

1. Draw a mural of Josh McBroom's one-acre farm (Fleischman, 1984).

2. Using halves of apples, tempera paint, and heavy construction paper, make apple prints (Kellogg, 1988).

3. Using leaves from apple trees, paper, and crayons, make leaf rubbings.

When immersed in the tall tales children will begin to formulate their own questions and ideas for projects and research. Take time to ask children what they would like to study. Allow them time to plan and implement their own projects and activities. The results will be absolutely amazing!

REFERENCES

Cohen, C.L. (1985). *Sally Ann Thunder Ann Whirlwind Crockett*. New York: Greenwillow.

Dewey, A. (1988). *The tea squall*. New York: Greenwillow.

Fleischman, S. (1984). *McBroom tells a lie*. Boston: Little, Brown.

Gleeson, B. (1988). *Pecos Bill*. Hong Kong: Rabbit Ear's Books.

Keats, E.J. (1965). *John Henry: An American legend*. New York: Pantheon.

Kellogg, S. (1986). *Pecos Bill*. New York: Morrow.

Kellogg, S. (1988). *Johnny Appleseed*. New York: Morrow.

Osborne, M.P. (1991). *American tall tales*. New York: Scholastic.

Purdy, C. (1985). *Iva Dunnit and the big wind*. New York: Dial.

Zorn, S. (1992). *Classic American folk tales*. Philadelphia: Courage.

Promoting world peace and understanding: The Batchelder Award-winning books

Rosie Webb Joels
Jackie K. Barnette

VOLUME 51, NUMBER 4, DECEMBER 1997/JANUARY 1998

Teachers face many challenges, among them selecting quality literature that presents worthwhile content and student appeal. The task becomes increasingly daunting, since publishers annually distribute more than 2,000 new children's titles considered to be of literary quality. Professionals' critical review of a fraction of these seems unrealistic. Literary award winners, however, offer teachers and librarians resources judged earlier by established evaluative criteria. We describe here a significant literary award and suggest some personal connections that make these works relevant for today's youth.

The Mildred L. Batchelder Award has been presented since 1968 to the U.S. publisher of the most outstanding children's book originally published in a foreign language in a foreign country whose English translation is subsequently published in the United States. The award en-courages international exchange of superior children's books in the belief that "interchange of children's books between countries, through translation, influences communication between the peoples of the countries" (American Library Association, 1987).

One finds varied genre, style, and themes in Batchelder Award winners. Many have a European setting during a world war. Despite most U.S. readers' lack of experience (across time and space) with the settings, kinship and connectedness are acutely established. The works achieve this through main characters (none above the teen years), feelings and frustrations, experiences, and desires that the creators so artfully produce.

It should be noted that the themes, events, and conditions described in the Batchelder Award winners may be considered painfully realistic and that teacher judgment on suitability for a particular

The Mildred L. Batchelder Award winners

Award year	U.S. publisher	Title	Author	Translator
1996	Houghton Mifflin	*The Lady With the Hat*	Uri Orlev	Hillel Halkin
1995	Dutton	*The Boys From St. Petri*	Bjarne Reuter	Anthea Bell
1994	Farrar, Straus & Giroux	*The Apprentice*	Pilar Molina Llorente	Robin Longshaw
1993	No award			
1992	Houghton Mifflin	*The Man From the Other Side*	Uri Orlev	Hillel Halkin
1991	Dutton	*A Hand Full of Stars*	Rafik Schami	Rika Lesser
1990	Dutton	*Buster's World*	Bjarne Reuter	Anthea Bell
1989	Lothrop, Lee & Shepard	*Crutches*	Peter Härtling	Elizabeth D. Crawford
1988	Macmillan/ Margaret K. McElderry	*If You Didn't Have Me*	Ulf Nilsson	George Blecher & Lone Thygesen-Blecher
1987	Lothrop, Lee & Shepard	*No Hero for the Kaiser*	Rudolph Frank	Patricia Crampton
1986	Creative Education	*Rose Blanche*	Christopher Gallaz & Roberto Innocenti	Martha Coventry & Richard Graglia
1985	Houghton Mifflin	*The Island on Bird Street*	Uri Orlev	Hillel Halkin
1984	Viking	*Ronia, the Robber's Daughter*	Astrid Lindgren	Patricia Crampton
1983	Lothrop, Lee & Shepard	*Hiroshima No Pika*	Toshiko Toshi Maruki	Kurita-Bando Literary Agency
1982	Bradbury	*The Battle Horse*	Harry Kullman	George Blecher & Lone Thygesen-Blecher
1981	Morrow	*The Winter When Time Was Frozen*	Els Pelgrom	Maryka Rudnick & Raphael Rudnick
1980	Dutton	*The Sound of the Dragon's Feet*	Aliki Zei	Edward Fenton
1979	HBJ	*Rabbit Island*	Jörg Steiner	Ann Conrad Lammers
(two winners)	Watts	*Konrad*	Christine Nöstlinger	Anthea Bell
1978	No award			
1977	Atheneum	*The Leopard*	Cecil Bodker	Gunnar Poulsen
1976	Walck	*The Cat and Mouse Who Shared a House*	Ruth Hürlimann	Anthea Bell
1975	Crown	*An Old Tale Carved Out of Stone*	A. Linevski	Maria Polushkin
1974	Dutton	*Petros' War*	Aliki Zei	Edward Fenton
1973	Morrow	*Pulga*	S.R. Van Iterson	Alexander Code & Alison Code
1972	Holt	*Friedrich*	Hans Peter Richter	Edite Kroll
1971	Pantheon	*In the Land of Ur: The Discovery of Ancient Mesopotamia*	Hans Baumann	Stella Humphries
1970	Holt	*Wildcat Under Glass*	Aliki Zei	Edward Fenton
1969	Scribner	*Don't Take Teddy*	Babbis Friis-Baastad	Lise Somme McKinnon
1968	Knopf	*The Little Man*	Erich Kästner	James Kirkup

class is essential. It is likely, however, these books would be most appropriate for students in the intermediate grades and above.

REFERENCE

American Library Association. (1987). *The Mildred L. Batchelder Award* (descriptive brochure). Chicago: Author.

Choosing picture books about ecology

Audrey Rule
Joan Atkinson

VOLUME 47, NUMBER 7, APRIL 1994

Proper care of the earth is a topic vital to children's education today. Authors and illustrators of children's picture books have the challenge of informing children of the world's environmental problems without overwhelming them with doom and gloom. Elementary school teachers and librarians select and use these books to instill an attitude of caring in children and to motivate them to be problem solvers in matters involving the planet. To assist in this process, especially for teachers who practice literature-based instruction, we present an analysis of children's picture books with ecology themes.

Ecology-related picture books can be used to showcase the beauty in nature and the interdependence of life on earth. Books need to heighten concern for the environment by portraying problems realistically and helping children realize that they can be part of the solutions. As in all literature, ecology picture books should have story appeal, illustrations that enhance the text, nonstereotypic characters, and recognition of children's developmental needs.

We used three professional reference sources to help develop our annotated bibliography: (a) *A to Zoo: Subject Access to Children's Picture Books*, 3rd ed. 1989. Carolyn W. Lima and John A. Lima. Bowker. Subject heading, ecology, (b) *Children's Books in Print. Subject Guide.* 1991–1992. Bowker. Subject heading, ecology—fiction, and (c) *The Elementary School Library Collection: A Guide to Books and Other Media*, 18th ed. 1992. Lauren K. Lee and Gary D. Hoyle (Eds.). Brodart. Subject headings, ecology–fiction, and pollution–fiction.

We analyzed 30 picture books using criteria that took into account subject content, literary and artistic merit, and sensitivity to children's developmental needs. We rated books on 10 traits, 5 relating to presentation of the environmental message to children and 5 relating to quality of the text and illustrations. Ratings reflect content information and curricular usefulness, as well as literary and artistic concerns.

Within each category we assigned ratings on the following basis: (5) very positive, (4) positive, (3) marginal, (2) negative, (1) very negative. The categories are defined in Table 1; ratings for each book are presented in Table 2. Some of the best books we found to present important ecology themes to children are described briefly below.

Table 1
Scaling categories and criteria

1. **Nature appreciation**
   Assesses the degree to which the book depicts beauty and harmony in nature.

2. **Interrelatedness of nature**
   Demonstrates the need for people's cooperation with nature. Shows how actions of one living thing affect others.

3. **Realistic ecology problem**
   Presents an ecology problem in a realistic manner, without oversimplification or exaggeration. The effect of human choice on the situation is clear.

4. **Hope of solution**
   Assesses to what degree books convey a feeling of hope of a viable solution to the problem.

5. **Steps for a solution**
   Rates books on whether there were actions that help to solve the ecology problem, whether there were actions that could be taken immediately by the reader, and whether at least some of the solutions could be realistically implemented by children.

6. **Positive tone**
   Emphasizes being effective in solving the problem rather than assigning blame or being "right." Positive and appropriate behaviors are emphasized, and the tone does not induce fear. Children are respectfully viewed as persons capable of thinking critically and logically.

7. **Nonstereotypic portrayals**
   Evaluates the degree to which stereotyping is avoided in treatment of either issues or characters.

8. **Appropriate illustrations**
   Assesses the degree to which illustrations enhance the text.

9. **Story appeal**
   Evaluates the characters and indicates whether the story has appropriate action, suspense, pace, and outcome.

10. **Developmental appropriateness**
    Rates books on the appropriateness of concepts, vocabulary, and sentence structure.

Table 2
Ratings for selected children's books with ecology themes

	Ratings given to each book on 10 traits									
	Presentation of environmental message					Quality of text and illustrations				
Major ecology themes and children's books containing them	Nature appreciation	Interrelatedness of nature	Realistic ecology problem	Hope for a solution	Steps for a solution	Positive tone	Nonstereotypical portrayals	Appropriate illustrations	Story appeal	Developmental appropriateness
Endangered species										
Journey of the Red-Eyed Tree Frog	5	5	5	5	4	5	4	5	4	4
Urban Roosts	4	4	4	4	4	5	5	4	4	4
The Lorax	4	5	5	3	3	4	3	4	5	5
Hey! Get Off Our Train	4	5	3	3	2	4	3	4	4	5
June Mountain Secret	4	4	3	4	4	4	4	4	3	3
Noah's Ark	4	4	3	3	2	4	2	4	3	3
As Dead as a Dodo	5	5	5	1	2	1	1	4	1	1
Destruction of habitats, forests										
The Great Kapok Tree	5	5	5	3	3	5	4	5	4	3
Save That Raccoon!	4	5	5	5	4	4	4	3	4	4
Where the Forest Meets the Sea	5	4	4	3	2	4	4	5	4	3
The True Story of Smoky the Bear	4	4	3	4	5	4	3	2	2	5
Were You a Wild Duck, Where Would You Go?	5	5	4	2	2	2	3	4	3	2
The Jungle Is My Home	4	4	2	1	1	1	1	2	1	2
Pollution										
Just a Dream	4	5	5	5	5	5	4	5	5	5
A River Ran Wild	5	5	5	5	4	5	5	5	3	4
The Seal and the Slick	4	5	5	5	5	5	5	4	5	5
The Wump World	4	5	5	3	2	3	2	4	5	5
The Great Fish	4	5	4	3	2	3	3	4	3	1
The Caboose Who Got Loose	4	4	3	2	1	3	2	4	3	5
And Still the Turtle Watched	4	4	3	3	2	1	1	4	2	2
The Last Free Bird	4	5	3	1	1	1	1	2	1	1
Land use and overpopulation										
Brother Eagle, Sister Sky	5	5	5	4	4	5	4	5	4	3
If I Built a Village	4	4	3	5	4	5	4	4	3	5
The Little House	4	4	4	2	1	3	4	4	5	5
Farewell to Shady Glade	4	4	3	2	1	3	3	4	5	5
Mr. Mole	4	4	4	2	1	3	3	4	4	5
Window	4	5	5	1	1	2	2	5	4	3
Fly, Homer, Fly	4	4	2	2	1	3	3	4	4	5
Heron Street	4	4	3	1	1	2	3	4	3	3
The Land of Gray Wolf	4	4	3	3	2	1	1	4	2	3

Rating scale: 5 = very good, 3 = marginal, 1 = very poor

Endangered species

Dr. Seuss's *The Lorax* (1971), a rhyming fantasy and children's favorite for over 20 years, still advocates powerfully for preserving the environment. The story is told by the Once-ler, now a recluse, who had arrived years earlier in the forest of Truffula Trees exclaiming happily,

> The touch of their tufts
> was much softer than silk.
> And they had the sweet smell
> of fresh butterfly milk.

Greed possessed the Once-ler, who chopped down Truffula Trees, knitted Thneeds, and became wealthy. Despite warnings from the Lorax, who spoke "for the trees," the Once-ler persisted. Soon animals, birds, fish, and even all the Truffula Trees disappeared. Now alone, the Once-ler shares his story with a curious boy. As the Lorax lifted himself away through a hole in the smog, he left a pile of rocks with a word, "UNLESS." Unless what? Children may try to guess. Then Dr. Seuss tells them:

> You're in charge of the last of the Truffula Seeds.
> And Truffula Tress are what everyone needs.
> Plant a new Truffula. Treat it with care.
> Give it clean water. And feed it fresh air.
> Grow a forest. Protect it from axes that hack.
> Then the Lorax
> and all of his friends
> may come back.

Though the story lacks subtlety in presenting the environmental message, its nonsense words and rhyming sounds appeal to children, as do Dr. Seuss's bold, animated, and humorous drawings.

A talking animal fantasy about endangered plants and animals is *Journey of the Red-Eyed Tree Frog* (1991) by Tanis Jordan. Tiny tree frog Hops-a-Bit is warned that his Central American forest home is in danger of destruction and that he needs to seek the counsel of the Great Wise Toad, who lives in the heart of the Amazon rain forest. After an arduous journey in which many unusual animals help him find the way, he approaches the "awesome creature" and receives and answer about the earth's future: "You have come about the problem of the people. The world belongs to all creatures, including the people. But too many people want it all for themselves. We do not have the power to stop them."

Despite this somber truth, Hops-a-Bit learns that his journey has a purpose: "What you have done will make more people want to share, especially children. They can make a better future for all the world's creatures."

Despite the didacticism of the text, illustrations of the exotic and endangered animals in their habitats will enthrall children, who may then be asked to brainstorm what children can do to take better care of the world.

An informational book that helps children think about adaptation of displaced animals to new environments is *Urban Roosts* (1990) by Barbara Bash. The story has no human characters but holds children's interest by picturing birds nesting in places familiar to city children, such as on ledges, under bridges, in lampposts or traffic signal lights, and on statues. Without anthropomorphizing, the illustrations suggest the ingenuity of birds in locating habitats suitable for survival and protection of the young. Children may be asked to look out for places around their school and near their homes where birds might safely build nests.

Destruction of habitats, particularly forests

Several picture books raise children's consciousness of the threat posed by distraction of woodlands and forests. In the poetic fantasy *The Great Kapok Tree* (Cherry, 1990), it is the Amazon rain forest that is in danger. A woodcutter tires as he chops on a massive kapok tree and eventually falls asleep beneath it. One by one the forest creatures whisper in his ear, begging him to think about them and about the future before he fells the tree. The book's endpapers provide a map of the world's tropical rain forests and picture many of the unusual species who live in them; illustrations throughout depict the beauty of the forest.

After reading, children could categorize the reasons given to the woodcutter according to whether they affect the future of the forest creatures or of children like themselves, in their homes and schools far away from the rain forests.

Where the Forest Meets the Sea (1987) by Jeannie Baker is a simply told first-person narrative of a child who travels with his father by boat into a coastal Australian tropical rain forest. He imagines aboriginal children and extinct animals who inhabited the forest for millions of years. His father promises that they will return, but the child wonders as his imagination builds resort hotels on the beach, "Will the forest still be here when we come back?"

Especially effective in enhancing the story are the illustrations, which are relief collages made of such materials as modeling clay, paper, textured fabrics, preserved natural materials, and paints. The book leads naturally to a discussion of reasons for forest destruction and whether destroyed forests could ever be replaced.

Pollution

Many delightful picture books depict the causes, effects, and measures for prevention of pollution. The dream fantasy *Just a Dream* (1990) by Chris Van Allsburg tells of Walter, a litterer who sneers at a friend's enjoyment of planting a tree as her birthday present and anticipates a future alive with robots and machines. That night his bed flies into the future, and Walter sees the garbage dumps, smog, traffic snarls, and land waste that result from people's demands for more and more machines. Walter arises the next morning with a plan to go "back to the future" by recycling, picking up his trash, and planting a tree of his own.

In the bold, colorful illustrations animals contrast with machines. The book seems to pose the question, "Would you rather have something alive or something manufactured for companionship in your future?"

A River Ran Wild (1992) by Lynne Cherry, an antipollution story that combines history and native folklore, traces the Nashua River from a time of pristine beauty to its pollution with stench and filth and eventually to its reclamation as "River with the Pebbled Bottom." Although most characters are adults, the focus is on the river and the children and animals who enjoy it when it is clean. A natural response to the book is "What can I do to keep rivers I enjoy clean and usable?"

In *The Wump World* (1970), a humorous fantasy by Bill Peet, the simple and charming wumps dive underground when the Pollutians from outer space invade their planet with thundering, smoke-belching machines. After the Wump World is destroyed, the Pollutians board their spaceships and zoom away, and the wumps ascend from their caves to walk the silent freeways filled with heaps of waste. Eventually they see a lone grassy meadow in which they wump for joy. Peet's ending, "In time the green growth would wind its way up through the rubble. But the Wump World would never be quite the same," invites children to consider what in the Wump World will never be quite the same again.

Land use and overpopulation

Decisions about land use hover in the futures of today's children, as population growth makes more demands on existing resources and encourages further clearing of the wilderness. Many picture books encourage children to question land use.

Brother Eagle, Sister Sky (1991), illustrated by Susan Jeffers, offers an eloquent plea from a Northwest Indian chief, Chief Seattle of the Susquamish, to think about the interrelatedness of all life:

> How can you buy the sky?
> How can you own the rain and the wind?
> My mother told me,
> Every part of this earth is sacred to our
>   people.
> Every one needle. Every sandy shore.
> Every mist in the dark woods.
> Every meadow and humming insect.
> All are holy in the memory of our people.

The message is powerful despite questions about the adaptation of this speech of ambiguous origin and about the authenticity of Jeffers's tribal images to Susquamish culture. The text is poetic, and the illustrations help to tell the story of European settlers who moved onto the land and changed it dramatically by clearcutting forests, dotting hillsides with utility poles, slaughtering buffalo, and taming the wild horses. Jeffers leaves the reader with hope, however. Chief Seattle says,

> All things are connected like the blood
>   that unites us.
> We did not weave the web of life,
> We are merely a strand within it.
> Whatever we do to the web, we do to ourselves.

One illustration shows a modern family planting seedlings on a hillside littered with stumps of trees; in the foreground is a beautiful spider web. As the family leaves the hillside, the boy looks over his shoulder and imagines that native peoples are watching and smiling.

A fantasy that helps children think about changing landscapes is *The Little House* (1942), a children's classic and Caldecott award winner by Virginia Lee Burton. Originally built in the country, the little house is slowly engulfed by the city and made sad and lonely by the never ending noise of traffic and the realization that she has become dirty and shabby. Then she is rescued by the great-great-granddaughter of the man who originally built her and is moved to the countryside.

Burton's endpapers show the technological progress of the times, as means of transportation change from horse, to buggy, to bicycle, to streetcar, and finally to automobile and truck. Children may be asked to imagine the changes the house or apartment they live in will see over the next hundred years as changes occur around it.

The theme of moving to a new home to escape overpopulation appears in many picture books. In *Heron Street* (Turner, 1989), set in Colonial American times, settlers crowd into town and wildlife flee. The story's use of sounds that mimic those of grasses and birds appeals to children, even though there is a tone of sadness as goodbyes are being said. The adventuresome animals in Peet's fantasy *Farewell to Shady Glade* (1966) set out to find a new wilderness home when a bulldozer destroys their familiar surroundings. In the thought-provoking wordless book *Window* (Baker, 1991), people participate in an inevitable cycle of settling in woodlands, filling and polluting the land, and moving away to cut down more woodlands for new settlements. Older children may be asked to think about the problems of continuing this cycle and actions people might take to break it.

Conclusion

An annotated bibliography of the 30 titles we analyzed is appended. Among these titles is tremendous diversity in tone, message, type of illustration, and literary genre. Humorous treatments such as those of Bill Peet and Dr. Seuss entertain as they develop their ecology themes, while serious and thought-provoking books such as those by Jeannie Baker and Lynne Cherry evoke a more critical response. Several literary genres are represented, including the poetry of *Brother Eagle, Sister Sky*, the dream fantasy of *Just a Dream*, the wordless treatment in *Window*, and the nonfiction *Urban Roosts*.

Even books that do not rank positively in each area of evaluation have value, for the group as a whole provides balance in both concept and design. Teachers may ask children to compare and contrast the books on such measures as the degree to which children's actions contribute to solutions, the degree of hopefulness of the ending, whether children can identify with the book's characters, and the feelings evoked by the illustrations.

A sensitive teacher may use a book with a message of doom like *The Last Free Bird* (Stone, 1967) to help children assess what can be done to avert the extinction of species rather than to focus on the book's despairing ending. A skillful teacher may use books with stereotypic treatments of settlers as universally greedy and wasteful, as in *The Land of Gray Wolf* (Locker, 1991) and *And Still the Turtle Watched* (MacGill-Callahan, 1991), as discussion starters for questions like "Are native and rural peoples always noble and good?" and "Are settlers and city dwellers always thoughtless and mean?" By valuing a slow-moving but beautiful book such as *Were You a Wild Duck, Where Would You Go?* (Mendoza, 1990), a teacher may interest children in its significant message.

The diversity of available books offers many possibilities for use. We hope that teachers and students will find just the right books for their special needs and enjoyment.

Annotated bibliography of selected books with ecology themes

Baker, J. 1987. *Where the forest meets the sea.* New York: Greenwillow. A boy muses about past inhabitants and appreciates the fantastic forest on a beautiful island, but wonders if it will all be lost to land development. Creative collage illustrations with double exposures suggest ghostly past inhabitants.

Baker, J. 1991. *Window.* New York: Greenwillow. The view from a boy's window changes as natural countryside becomes crowded city. Wordless; imaginative collage illustrations.

Bash, B. 1990. *Urban roosts: Where birds nest in the city.* San Fransisco: Sierra Club. Birds find ingenious places to roost and nest in a city. Informational; has unusual perspectives and humor.

Burningham, J. 1990. *Hey! Get off our train.* New York: Crown Press. A boy and his stuffed dog take a bedtime dream world train ride across the earth collecting endangered animals. Funny ending when the boy's mother discovers one of these animals in the bathtub. Repetition of wording.

Burton, V. 1942. *The little house.* Boston: Houghton Mifflin. A little rural house becomes encompassed by the dirty, growing city but is later returned to the countryside where it can again watch the stars and changing seasons. Repetition of pictures and wording. Caldecott Medal.

Cherry, L. 1990. *The great kapok tree.* San Diego: Harcourt Brace Jovanovich. A woodcutter enters the jungle to fell the kapok tree, but defers to the wisdom of the forest inhabitants who visit him as he naps. Promotes critical thinking; colorful, varied perspectives in illustrations.

Cherry, L. 1992. *A river ran wild.* San Diego: Harcourt Brace Jovanovich. The Nashua River's environmental true story is told, for clean "River with a Pebbled Bottom" of the Indians, to polluted industrial sewer, and finally to restored, living waterway. Interesting vignettes in borders of illustrations.

Fischetto, L. 1991. *The jungle is my home.* Ill. L. Galli. New York: Viking. In fablelike fashion jungle animals endure a pitiful plight when humans destroy their home by clearcutting the forest. Flat, stereotyped anthropomorphized characters; depressing ending.

Freeman, D. 1974. *The seal and the slick.* New York: Viking. Two children free a young seal caught in an oil slick. Watercolor illustrations depict nonstereotyped characters.

Haley, G.E. 1971. *Noah's ark.* New York: Atheneum. A modern day Noah builds an ark to rescue animals from pollution. Clever environmental twist in retelling old Bible story.

Jeffers, S. 1991. *Brother Eagle, Sister Sky.* New York: Dial. Chief Seattle delivers this historic speech of respect for nature as he reluctantly resigns Indian lands. Poetic text and mystical illustrations.

(continued)

Annotated bibliography of selected books with ecology themes (continued)

Jordan, T. 1991. *Journey of the red-eyed tree frog*. New York: Green Tiger. A tree frog encounters native animals on his trip to ask the Great Wise Toad for help in saving the Amazon jungle from human destruction. Bold, colorful illustrations.

Kidd, N. 1991. *June mountain secret*. New York: HarperCollins. A girl and her father fish for rainbow trout, but release the fish unharmed so that it can be free. Informational book with labeled vocabulary.

Locker, T. 1991. *The land of Gray Wolf*. New York: Dial. A young brave sees Indian land degraded and ruined. Slow, sad, historical account.

MacGill-Callahan, S. 1991. *And still the turtle watched*. Ill. B. Moser. New York: Dial. Indians carve a stone turtle to watch over the children, but it is forgotten over time, vandalized, and finally rescued. Heavy-handed and stereotyped with adult viewpoint.

Mendoza, G. 1990. *Were you a wild duck, where would you go?* Ill. J. Osborn-Smith. New York: Stewart, Tabori & Chang. A mallard tells of the natural beauty and abundance on earth before human greed intervened and encourages children to save the environment. Delicate watercolor illustrations, poetic text, adult theme and style.

Miklowitz, G.D. 1978. *Save that raccoon!* Ill. by S. Tamara. San Diego: Harcourt Brace Jovanovich. A forest fire forces raccoon and other wildlife into the city where they cause destruction until captured and moved. Nonjudgemental treatment of problem.

Mizumura, K. 1971. *If I built a village*. New York: Crowell. A child ponders the animals and plants that would live in peace in a city he planned. Simple, boldly outlined illustrations; poetic.

Murschetz, L. 1972. *Mr. Mole*. Trans. D. Martin. New York: Prentice-Hall. Mr. Mole, uprooted from his peaceful meadow life by bulldozers, moves on to find a new field. Illustrated with bold, simple shapes.

Parnall, P. 1973. *The great fish*. New York: Doubleday. An Indian grandfather tells of the great salmon and life in harmony with nature until modern times where there is thoughtless pollution of streams. Stylized Indian art line drawings, adult theme and style.

Peet. B. 1966. *Farewell to Shady Glade*. Boston: Houghton Mifflin. Several animals hop a train when bulldozers destroy their meadow and ride on to a new country home. Humorous illustrations.

Peet, B. 1969. *Fly, Homer, fly*. Boston: Houghton Mifflin. A lonely farm pigeon goes to the city for adventure, but is disappointed to find urban life dirty, heartless, and dangerous. Suspense and cleverness in plot.

Peet, B. 1970. *The wump world*. Boston: Houghton Mifflin. The spunky, pudgy wumps live happily on a lush green planet until the Pollutians come from outer space and take over. Expressive, lovable characters; strong plot.

Peet, B. 1971. *The caboose who got loose*. Boston: Houghton Mifflin. Katy the Caboose longs to escape from the sooty engine and dirty city freight yards to live in the country. Rhyming text; humor and whimsy in illustrations.

Rice, P., & Mayle, P. 1981. *As dead as a dodo*. Ill. S. Rice. Boston: Godine. Human greed and negligence resulted in the extinction of 16 animals presented in this museumlike collection of portraits and sad, shameful stories.

Seuss, Dr. 1971. *The Lorax*. New York: Random House. A sadder but wiser Once-ler tells how he exploited and ruined the local environment in spite of the warnings of the Lorax. Nonsense sounds; assonance; strong plot; clever characters; humor.

Stone, A.H. 1967. *The last free bird*. New York: Prentice Hall. The last living bird gives a testimony of human greed, selfishness, and pollution of the earth. Sad, hopeless, adult theme.

(continued)

Annotated bibliography of selected books with ecology themes (continued)

Turner, A. 1989. *Heron Street*. Ill. L. Desimini. New York: Harper & Row. Wildlife flee a seaside marsh as it is developed into pasture land, then noisy city. Clever use of sounds in text; historical account.

Van Allsburg, C. 1990. *Just a dream*. Boston: Houghton Mifflin. A nightmarish trip into a polluted future motivates a boy to be concerned for the environment. Illustrations capture dream-like quality of text.

Watson, J.W. 1955. *The true story of Smoky the Bear*. Ill. F. Rojankovsky. Racine, WI: Western. A bear cub rescued from a forest blaze becomes a ranger who teaches children to prevent forest fires. Sentimental; anthropomorphized; dated.

Using children's books as an intervention for attention-deficit disorder

Beth Fouse
Jane Ann Morrison

Volume 50, Number 5, February 1997

The lives of children with attention-deficit disorder (ADD) and their families are significantly affected by the behaviors exhibited by these children. Medication, behavior modification, and cognitive-behavioral management interventions assist both the family and the child in handling primary ADD characteristics such as hyperactivity, impulsivity, and distractibility (Braswell & Bloomquist, 1991).

Some individuals with ADD frequently develop secondary problems with learning, self-esteem, and interpersonal relationships. It is difficult for these children and their families to accept and understand these obstacles.

Because attention-deficit disorder is an invisible disability, many adults in the young child's life believe the child could behave more appropriately if he or she would just try. Teachers in mainstream classrooms may have little experience with ADD and, therefore, have unrealistic expectations for these students. This, in turn, often sets the children up for failure. Children with ADD may begin to think that there is no point in trying because their efforts rarely seem to make a difference. They perceive themselves as inadequate students unable to compete satisfactorily with peers. Many of these children learn to "save face" by becoming class clowns or using noncompliance to mask their disabilities.

Young children with attention-deficit disorder wonder why school is so hard for them when it appears so easy for their classmates. Peers do not understand why teachers and others make modifications and adaptations for students with ADD. Some children challenge the fairness of providing modifications and accommodations to classmates with ADD. Rejection of children with ADD by peers often results.

The use of children's books may enable ADD students to develop a clearer understanding of themselves and their problems. "Children's literature illustrates that some of their favorite characters, if their lives had been real, would be suffering the same growing pains that they are experiencing" (Mercer & Mercer, 1989, p. 169). These books can be read aloud to children by parents, teachers, and/or counselors and can provide the opportunity to discuss personal problems and concerns. Issues that can be addressed are (a) how children with ADD differ from and are similar to others, (b) how to handle criticism, (c) how to develop an understanding of their strengths and weaknesses, and (d) how to develop study skills and learning strategies that will nurture both cognitive and social-emotional growth (VanTassel-Baska, 1990).

The use of children's books to promote social and emotional growth may involve the stages of identification, catharsis, and insight. In the *identification* stage, the child personally identifies with a character in the literature. Through *catharsis*, the child is able to express personal feelings and release emotional tensions related to his/her problem. During the third stage, *insight*, the child learns to integrate intellectual understanding with personal feelings (Hoagland, 1972; Hildreth & Candler, 1992). Halstead added a fourth stage, *universalization*, which "is the reader's recognition that difficulties and sense of difference are not his or hers alone" (VanTassel-Baska, 1994, p. 133). Young children develop a better understanding or awareness of their problems through empathy with the characters.

Oral reading and teacher- or counselor-led discussions of the books facilitate children's understanding of peers with ADD. Discussions may promote greater empathy and tolerance for the behaviors exhibited by children with ADD and may help them feel more accepted.

Book discussion should encourage children to talk through personal feelings in a nonthreatening way. The children can interject feelings and needs through the character. Frustrations and anger can be expressed and vented. Children recognize that they are not alone in the problems that they face and learn that it's okay to feel sad, hurt, or angry. Coping skills are developed as children model ways in which characters work through similar problems. These skills assist children in facing challenges and in maximizing their potential.

To work effectively with children who have ADD, parents and educators should be aware of the various books related to the topic of attention-deficit disorder (Moore, 1990). (See annotated list.)

Parents and educators should not expect immediate results from reading and discussing one book. For optimal results, there should be repeated readings and discussions of a variety of related books. Experience shows that the children should be exposed to several books with the same concepts. The more children read and internalize ideas from books, the more likely it is that there will be a positive impact on the children's attitudes and behaviors.

Annotated bibliography of books for children about attention-deficit disorder (ADD)

All Kinds of Minds. Mel Levine. Educator's Publishing Service, 1993. Ages 7–14
  This book demonstrates that different children have different kinds of minds. The feelings that the characters have because of their difficulties in school are discussed. One chapter addresses ADD.

Bad Mood Bear. John Richardson. Barron's, 1988. Ages 4–8
  A little bear woke up in a bad mood because he did not get enough sleep. He is unkind to his friends and rude to his Grandma and Grandpa. Mom and Dad make him take a nap. He wakes up in a good mood.

Don't Look at Me. Doris Sanford. Multnomah Press, 1986. Ages 5–12
  Patrick, a young boy who feels bad about himself, is the focus of this book. The ways that feeling different affects Patrick and how a pet lamb helps him to feel better about himself and to make friends are explored in this story.

Don't Feed the Monster on Tuesdays! The Children's Self-Esteem Book. Adolph Moser. Landmark Editions, 1991. Ages 4–10
  Children are provided with practical strategies for understanding their self-worth and for evaluating and strengthening their self-esteem.

Don't Pop Your Cork on Mondays! The Children's Anti-Stress Book. Adolph Moser. Landmark Editions, 1988. Ages 4–10
  The causes and effects of children's stress are explored. Techniques for dealing with everyday stress situations are presented through colorful cartoons.

Don't Rant and Rave on Wednesdays! The Children's Anger-Control Book. Adolph Moser. Landmark Editions, 1994. Ages 5–12
  The causes of anger are explored, and strategies that children can use for reducing anger and controlling behavior are provided.

Eagle Eyes: A Child's Guide to Paying Attention. Jeanne Gehret. Verbal Images Press, 1991. Ages 6–10
  Ben, a young boy with ADD, helps readers of all ages understand this disorder through practical suggestions for organization, social cues, and self-calming.

Eukee the Jumpy, Jumpy Elephant. Cliff Korman & Esther Trevino. Specialty Press, 1995. Ages 3–8
  Eukee, a bright, hyperactive, young elephant, helps children understand why he is so jumpy. Eukee demonstrates how he learns to help himself and improve his self-esteem.

Help Me Be Good Books. Joy Berry. Grolier Enterprises, 1988. Ages 4–8
  These books for children deal with the various behavior problems that young children exhibit. Titles include *Bad Sport, Being Bossy, Being Bullied, Being Careless, Being Destructive, Being Forgetful, Being Greedy, Being Lazy, Being Mean, Being Messy, Being Rude, Being Selfish, Being Wasteful, Breaking Promises, Cheating, Complaining, Disobeying, Fighting, Gossiping, Interrupting, Lying, Overdoing It, Showing Off, Snooping, Stealing, Tattling, Teasing, Throwing Tantrums,* and *Whining.*

If They Can Do It, We Can Too! Deephaven School's Learning Lab Students & M.H. Dinneen. Deaconess Press, 1992. Ages 5–12
  Eighteen students with learning differences write about famous people who needed to learn in different ways when they were growing up. The common theme throughout the essays is that if the famous people could be successful, so could they!

I'm Frustrated. Elizabeth Crary. Parenting Press, 1992. Ages 5–12
  Alex gets very frustrated when he has difficulty learning to roller skate. He comes to realize that there are many appropriate ways to handle his feelings.

(continued)

Annotated bibliography of books for children about attention-deficit disorder (ADD) (continued)

I'm Mad. Elizabeth Crary. Parenting Press, 1992. Ages 5–12
  Kate learns to deal with anger in appropriate ways, such as doing something physical and talking about her feelings, instead of having a temper tantrum and yelling.

I'm Proud. Elizabeth Crary. Parenting Press, 1992. Ages 5–12
  Self-affirmation is crucial to building self-esteem, and this book emphasizes that individuals can recognize the value of their own achievements, even when others do not provide external approval.

I'm Somebody Too. Jeanne Gehret. Verbal Images Press, 1992. Ages 9+
  Children and parents understand, through this book, the feelings of siblings who feel left out because of the attention that is sometimes focused on the child with a disability.

I Would If I Could: A Teenager's Guide to ADHD/Hyperactivity. Michael Gordon. GSI Publications, 1994. Ages 12–18
  Information is provided about ADHD while exploring its effect on family relationships, self-esteem, and friendships. The humorous approach makes it especially appropriate for adolescents.

Jumpin' Jake Settles Down. A Workbook for Active, Impulsive Kids. Lawrence Shapiro. The Center for Applied Psychology, 1994. Ages 5–10
  Impulsive children learn to stop and think before they act through the activities contained in this book about Jumpin' Jake, a hyperactive, impulsive frog.

Jumpin' Johnny Get Back to Work! A Child's Guide to ADHD/Hyperactivity. Spanish edition: Juan El Brincon De Nuevo a Tu Trabajo! Guia Para El Nino Con ADHD/Hyperactivity. Michael Gordon. GSI Publications, 1991. Ages 5–10
  Johnny, an inattentive and impulsive child, has difficulty at school and at home. The methods that his family and school use to make his life easier are shown.

Just Because I Am: A Child's Book of Affirmation. Lauren M. Payne. Free Spirit, 1994. Ages 4–8
  Although not specific to children with ADD, this book strengthens and supports a child's self-esteem with simple words and gentle, appealing illustrations. Children learn that they are special "just because I am." A Leader's Guide is also available to help children build self-esteem.

Kids Explore the Gifts of Children With Special Needs. Westridge Young Writers Workshop. John Muir Publications, 1994. Ages 8–16
  Written from a kid's point of view, this book profiles 10 young people with disabilities including a young boy with ADD.

Learning My Way: I'm a Winner! Judy H. Swenson & Roxane B. Kunz. Dillon, 1986. Ages 7–10
  The main character, Dan, talks about his difficulties in school. The book explains how his learning difficulty and hyperactivity were diagnosed and the ways in which his education program helped to make learning easier.

Learning to Slow Down and Pay Attention. Kathleen Nadeau & Ellen Dixon. Chesapeake Publications, 1993. Ages 6–14
  Written for children and illustrated with cartoons, this book helps children identify problems and explains how their parents, teachers, and doctor can help. Paying attention, managing feelings, getting more organized, and learning to problem-solve are addressed.

Making the Grade. An Adolescent's Struggle With ADHD. Spanish edition: Como Pasar De Grado. Roberta N. Parker. Impact Publications, 1992. Ages 9–14
  Jim Jerome's difficulties with self-control and inattention create problems for him as he enters junior high school. Jim's parents, teachers, and health professionals assist him in learning about ADD and in developing strategies to help himself.

(continued)

Annotated bibliography of books for children about attention-deficit disorder (ADD) (continued)

My Brother's a World Class Pain: A Sibling's Guide to ADHD. Michael Gordon. GSI Publications, 1992. Ages 6–12

The nature of ADHD and siblings' feelings about the demands placed on other family members when children with ADHD are part of the family are explored in this selection.

Otto Learns About His Medicine: A Story About Medication for Hyperactive Children. Matthew Galvin. Brunner/Mazel, 1988. Ages 5–10

Otto, a red car, exhibits characteristics of ADHD and must visit a special mechanic who prescribes medicine to control his hyperactive behavior. Although medication is prescribed, personal responsibility for behavior is still emphasized.

Putting on the Brakes: A Young People's Guide to Understanding Attention Deficit Hyperactivity Disorder (ADHD). Patricia O. Quinn & Judith M. Stern. Brunner/Mazel, Magination Press, 1991. Ages 8–12

Children with ADHD are given a sense of control and a feeling that they can resolve problems. Students are reassured that the problems they face are not unique to them.

Shelley, the Hyperactive Turtle. Deborah Moss. Woodbine House, 1989. Ages 4–7

Shelley, a young turtle, and his family face the challenges presented by his hyperactivity. The book explains hyperactivity for children with ADHD, their siblings, and their friends.

Slam Dunk: A Young Boy's Struggle with ADD. Roberta N. Parker. Impact Publications, 1993. Ages 8–12

Classroom accommodations and behavioral and medical interventions for Toby, a fifth-grade student with a problem paying attention, are discussed. The fictional story is followed by a question-and-answer section by H.C. Parker.

Sometimes I Drive My Mom Crazy, But I Know She's Crazy About Me. Lawrence Shapiro. The Center for Applied Psychology, 1993. Ages 5–10

The difficult issues confronted daily by children with ADD are addressed. Behavior programs, educational management, and medication information are presented by a young boy with ADD who has developed a sense of self-worth by effectively dealing with his problems.

The Boy on the Bus. Diana Loski. Writer's Press, 1994. Ages 6–10

Margo is upset about having to ride on the bus with Corey, a young boy with ADD. As she learns more about Corey and ADD, she comes to accept him as he is.

The Boys and Girls' Book of Dealing with Feelings. Eric Duglokinski. The Feelings Factory, 1993. Ages 5–10

Colorful illustrations are used to describe strategies for coping with other people's reactions. It teaches four basic steps for dealing with such feelings as sadness, fear, and anger.

The Don't Give-Up Kid. Jeanne Gehret. Verbal Images Press, 1990. Ages 5–12

Alex, a child with a learning disability, realizes that his hero, Thomas Edison, faced similar problems throughout his childhood. Like Edison, he learns to try new solutions until he succeeds at his dream of creating new things.

The Survival Guide for Kids with LD. Gary Fisher & Rhoda Cummings. Free Spirit, 1990. Ages 8–12.

Although written specifically for students with learning disabilities, this book has good information for students with ADD. Appropriate sections include dealing with feelings, getting along better in school, reacting to teasing, tips for making friends, and getting along at home.

When Emily Woke Up Angry. Riana Duncan. Barron's, 1989. Ages 4–10

A young girl named Emily woke up angry and didn't know how to deal with her anger. She encountered many different animals and tried their methods of dealing with anger until she found one that worked for her.

Family and friends generally react more favorably to the improved behavior. Therefore, books that promote positive attitudes and behaviors serve as effective tools for the development of a child's social-emotional well-being.

REFERENCES

Braswell, L., & Bloomquist, M.L. (1991). *Cognitive-behavioral therapy with ADHD Children*. New York: The Guilford Press.

Hildreth, B.L., & Candler, A. (1992). Learning about learning disabilities through general public literature. *Intervention in School and Clinic, 27*, 293–296.

Hoagland, J. (1972). Bibliotherapy: Aiding children in personality development. *Elementary English, 49*, 390–394.

Mercer, C.D., & Mercer, A.R. (1989). *Teaching students with learning problems*. New York: Merrill.

Moore, C. (1990). *A reader's guide for parents of children with mental, physical, or emotional disabilities*. Rockville, MD: Woodbine House.

VanTassel-Baska, J. (Ed.) (1990). *A practical guide to counseling the gifted in a school setting* (2nd ed.). Reston, VA: Council for Exceptional Children.

VanTassel-Baska, J. (1994). *Comprehensive curriculum for gifted learners*. Boston: Allyn & Bacon.

Readers' workshop in a kindergarten classroom

John W. Bryan

VOLUME 52, NUMBER 5, FEBRUARY 1999

In my first-year experience in a kinder-garten classroom, I quickly introduced DEAR (Drop Everything And Read) time to both of my half-day classes the first week of school. Because we have special classes such as art, music, library, and gym, I was limited to a 1-hour 40-minute instruction period. Regardless, within the first month of school, DEAR time went from 5 minutes daily to 20 minutes. During DEAR time, the children selected a book, plopped down on a pillow, and read. I felt it my duty to plop down right beside them as an adult model enjoying literacy. Many times during this period, I would be asked to lap read to an individual or a small group of children. In general, my children tended to share and read in groups; very few children chose to read alone. Indeed, I found that this reading time became a very important and valuable time for social as well as academic growth.

DEAR time became an integral part of my reading curriculum. It allowed me to express my enthusiasm and love of books while reading, expose and read a picture book daily to children, provide children independent time to read books on their own, and encourage children to socialize and enjoy reading together. I believe that I accomplished these goals, but something was missing.

Mid-year, when I finally felt that I had a grasp on my students' abilities, I was becoming nervously aware of children who had very little letter recognition, children who were readers, and children who were at emerging reading levels and needed direct instruction to nurture continued growth. With the limited time I had in kindergarten, when could I individualize or work with small groups? I managed to implement an individualized reading program for my confident readers, but what about my other students?

Why would a kindergarten teacher want readers' workshop?

It wasn't until I attended Susan Thomas's 2-day lecture on readers' work-shop that I realized that I was missing time to work with individuals and small groups, time to monitor student progress regardless of levels, and a means to harness my students' socialization skills and synthesize higher thinking skills. I was very excited and eager to transform my DEAR time into a readers' workshop when I returned to my classroom. I felt that readers' workshop was a solution to those nagging deficiencies that I perceived with DEAR time.

Week 1: Set-up. On Monday, I informed my students that we would not be having DEAR time anymore (the students responded with moans and booing). I used a pie chart to introduce the readers' workshop time setup to my students; I used the analogy of a large pepperoni pizza—terms that they could understand. I explained to them that I get a small piece of that pizza (5 minutes) to work with the whole class, a small group, or an individual. During this time, I could not be disturbed unless blood was involved (they thought this was funny!). The majority of the pizza belonged to them for reading. The rest of the pizza (5 minutes) was theirs as well as a time to share thoughts about a book read. They agreed that they liked this and were anxious to shop for books. I didn't allow them to shop yet. I wanted to be certain that I patiently took my time to model, demonstrate, and practice correct procedure for our readers' workshop.

The next day, I explained once again about the setup for readers' workshop. I had purchased small plastic baskets in which I placed my emergent reader books. In addition, I have an extensive picture book library of my own from which

students can always choose. I also purchased gallon-size plastic bags to be used as shopping bags.

During the remainder of the week, I demonstrated how students must read one familiar, shared book (we've read many emergent reader books together) and one book of their choice. I showed them exactly how to fill their shopping bags, where to place them, and how to clean up afterwards. I reviewed proper book handling skills for individual and big books. Students then practiced the routine several times without reading the books. It wasn't until week 2 that we actually began to read books during readers' workshop. Looking back, all of the practice and preparation that first week paid off—students knew what was expected of them, and things ran smoothly during the workshop.

Week 2: Smooth operations. The first official day of readers' workshop went perfectly. The students knew the routine: there were no interruptions, the noise level was well maintained, and cleanup was a breeze. During the first part of readers' workshop, I decided to work with the class as a whole. I read two books that I had read before and were class favorites: *Owen* and *Julius, Baby of the World* (Henkes, 1993 & 1990). The kids easily related to these books so I decided to scaffold and organize their knowledge of the books using a T-chart. As a large group, we filled in the chart using different characters from the books. The students caught on and really got into the different dilemmas that each character faced. They were eager to discuss these problems with their neighbors. Good literature promotes discussion. Before readers' workshop, when I read a book, it was my expectation that children sit silently as I read...discussion was for afterward. What I learned from this week is that it is absolutely necessary to allow children to share their understandings of literature as we read together. Children predicted outcomes, related characters and events to their own lives, and engaged in higher level thinking. What an eye-opener!

Week 3: The alphabet gang. I was feeling pretty confident by the third week. I felt that the children had made a very smooth transition from DEAR time to readers' workshop. I was thrilled to hear several boys singing books as they read them.

At this time, I wanted to focus on working with those children who knew 8 or fewer letters. I used a technique that Tom Donovan, a reading teacher, gave me. I passed out an alphabet booklet that had letters and representational pictures for each letter (Apple—A). In a small group and using a "chunking" technique, we only focused on the letters *A* through *D* for the entire week. Children had to touch the letter, say it, and say the pictured item. Afterward, I had the children practice these four letters using "back writing." They loved it. As they were practicing, I began to monitor and read with the remainder of the students.

It was during this week that the children began to share something about the book they had read. For the most part, I had to elicit responses from the children: "What was your favorite part of the book?" "Would you recommend this book?" I tried to refrain from asking factual questions and aimed for higher level thinking skills.

Week 4: A technological boom. At this point I was extremely pleased with the way things were going with readers' workshop. What else could I possibly add to make it better? I got the answer when looking through the Sunday newspaper advertisements. A local electronics store had a sale on personal cassette players. I bought six. Placing the cassette players in "shopping bags," I turned them into mini listening centers by adding a different picture book and cassette to each. I felt this would help supplement the lap reading when I was working with groups. The mini listening centers were a huge success, and each week I changed the stories.

During week 4, I focused on expanding my students' reading repertoire of emergent reader books. At the beginning of readers' workshop, I introduced and read several predictable, highly repetitive books so that students would have more choices when selecting the one book that they knew how to read. I continued to share and read daily from big books, and I found that these were the most popular books chosen by students when shopping.

I worked with a homogeneous group of children who were flourishing as emergent readers. I found that working with this group during the week enabled them to excel. We focused on two new sight words each week, and I found this group able to transfer this new knowledge quickly to other books.

My students seem to be quite content and happy during readers' workshop. I discovered just how successful this workshop was going when I was out 2 days for a math workshop. When I returned, the substitute had written that both days the classes didn't get around to doing readers' workshop (apparently, they ran out of time). I asked both groups how they liked the substitute, and unanimously they said they didn't like her because she wouldn't let them have readers' workshop. Wow!

Why implement a kindergarten readers' workshop?

I feel that readers' workshop has been a great success! I wish only that I had known about it sooner. By transforming my DEAR time into the workshop, I feel that I was able to accomplish all my goals: (a) making time for quality interaction with all students; (b) addressing the needs of all students, regardless of level or ability; and (c) giving my students the chance to voice literary opinions and share their enjoyment within our family of literacy learners.

To me, the most successful aspects of the workshop were the group time, the listening centers, and the quality of strategies that I am able to work on with children.

In the future, I will introduce my new students to DEAR time just as I did this year. After several weeks, I will transform this time into readers' workshop. By starting the workshop during the second month of school, I think that I will be able to assess and start working with groups right away. I plan on stockpiling books on tapes, and I would like to make cloth shopping bags since I plan on making readers' workshop a staple of my kindergarten class.

Caldecott Medal books and readability levels: Not just "picture" books

Julia Chamberlain
Dorothy Leal

VOLUME 52, NUMBER 8, MAY 1999

According to an ancient Chinese proverb, "One picture is worth more than a thousand words." If this is the case, what better way might we engage a child's interest in reading a story than by combining it with first-rate illustrations? Today's teachers want to help students select books that will spark interest while providing a comfortable readability level. The challenge is how to do this. The prestigious Caldecott Medal for excellence in illustration has already done part of this work by providing us with a list of noteworthy picture books. This article is aimed at offering further help by supplying an overview of Caldecott readability levels along with some suggestions for using the books.

Although beautifully illustrated books grab everyone's immediate interest, from the youngest child through adults, if the accompanying texts are not accessible, the books will be of little use to students.

Determining which book matches a particular student's reading ability can be difficult. To make that task easier for teachers, we have evaluated the readability levels of each of the Caldecott Medal-winning books published from the award's inception in 1938 through the 1998 winner.

The readability level, described as "the difficulty of the content, vocabulary, and structure of a given book" (Shafritz, Koeppe, & Soper, 1988, p. 385), is a key factor in the appropriate selection of books that children can read and enjoy. The focus for this readability study of Caldecott award books is on the structure and level of understanding required to engage the text in these books.

As in our parallel Newbery study (Leal & Chamberlain-Solecki, 1998), the Fry readability formula (Fry, 1977) used in this study, is based on the average (a) number of sentences in three 100-word passages and (b) number of syllables in the same passages. The average of the three passages for both number of sentences and number of syllables is then charted on Fry's graph to determine grade-level readability. We randomly selected passages to evaluate at the beginning, middle, and end of each of the books.

We knew that readability outcomes vary greatly depending on the passages selected because readability levels for conversational passages are generally lower than for descriptive writing. But, because the Fry readability formula was designed for use with chapter books, we ran into some new problems with the Caldecott books.

First, the fact that several of the Caldecott books have too few pages or too few words for such an evaluation might skew some of the results. For example, in 10 of the Caldecott books the total word count for each was 400 or less, barely enough words to complete three 100-word passages. Further, 3 of those 10 books had only enough words to evaluate one 100-word passage. Since three passages were not available, the readability level was taken from that sample alone. Second, 1992's winner *Tuesday*, has only 18 words with 32 syllables in a total of four sentences. Since this could not be charted, it was scored as a zero.

Some interesting findings

After determining the individual readability level for each of the Caldecott books, an average grade level for the 61 books was computed. Despite the fact that these are often considered picture books, the overall grade-level readability average for all Caldecott books is 4.75. It is interesting to note that the average readability level has changed over time. From 1938 to 1978 the readability by decade averages from 5.0 to 5.6, whereas, in the last two decades the averages are a full grade lower: 4.3 and 4.2, respectively. Grade-level findings for each of the Caldecott books are reported in the Table.

The Caldecott criteria state that the award is for "a picture book for children... that essentially provides the child with a visual experience (which has) a collective unity of story-line, theme, or concept" (Association for Library Service to Children, 1995, p. 5). The definition also states that the book must display "respect for children's understandings, abilities, and appreciations." As with the Newbery criteria, children are defined as "persons of ages up to and including fourteen." Examination of the Table shows that 34% of the books' reading levels fall in the first-through fourth-grade level, 28% are at the fifth-grade level, and the remaining 38% are at the sixth- and seventh-grade level. Thus the Caldecott books appear to primarily cover reading levels for the elementary school years.

However, if one assumes age 14 to be equivalent to ninth grade, it indicates that there are only a few high-quality "picture story" books for the older grades. That is the inverse of the problem found in the Newbery Medal books, where only one book was at a fourth-grade reading level and none were lower. Among Caldecott books, there are none at the eighth- and

Readability levels for Caldecott Medal books

Award year	Title	Illustrator	Author	Readability level	Cultural focus
1938	Animals of the Bible, a Picture Book	Dorothy P. Lathrop	Text Selected by Helen Dean Fish	7	
1939	Mei Li	Thomas Handforth	Thomas Handforth	5	Chinese
1940	Abraham Lincoln	Ingri & Edgar Parin D' Aulaire	Ingri & Edgar Parin D' Aulaire	6	
1941	They Were Strong and Good	Robert Lawson	Robert Lawson	6	
1942	Make Way for Ducklings	Robert McCloskey	Robert McCloskey	5	
1943	The Little House	Virginia Lee Burton	Virginia Lee Burton	6	
1944	Many Moons	Louis Slobodkin	James Thurber	5	
1945	Prayer for a Child*	Elizabeth Orton Jones	Rachel Field	5	
1946	The Rooster Crows	Maud & Miska Petersham	Maud & Miska Petersham	5	
1947	The Little Island	Leonard Weisgard	Golden MacDonald, pseud. (Margaret Wise Brown)	6	
1948	White Snow, Bright Snow	Roger Duvoisin	Alvin Tresselt	6	
1949	The Big Snow	Berta & Elmer Hader	Berta & Elmer Hader	5	
1950	Song of the Swallows	Leo Politi	Leo Politi	4	Spanish
1951	The Egg Tree	Katherine Milhous	Katherine Milhous	3	
1952	Finders Keepers	Nicolas, pseud. (Nicholas Mordvinoff)	Will, pseud. (William Lipkind)	2	
1953	The Biggest Bear	Lynd Ward	Lynd Ward	5	
1954	Madeline's Rescue	Ludwig Bemelmans	Ludwig Bemelmans	3	
1955	Cinderella, or the Little Glass Slipper	Marcia Brown	Translated from Charles Perrault by Marcia Brown	5	French
1956	Frog Went A-Courtin'+	Feodor Rojankovsky	Retold by John Lagstaff	3	
1957	A Tree Is Nice+	Marc Simont	Janice May Udry	1	
1958	Time of Wonder	Robert McCloskey	Robert McCloskey	7	
1959	Chanticleer and the Fox	Barbara Cooney	Adapted from Chaucer's Canterbury Tales by B. Cooney	6	Old English Tale
1960	Nine Days to Christmas	Marie Hall Ets	Marie Hall Ets & Aurora Labastida	6	Mexican
1961	Babouska and the Three Kings	Nicolas Sidjakov	Ruth Robbins	4	Russian
1962	Once a Mouse+	Marcia Brown	Retold by Marcia Brown	5	Indian Folklore
1963	The Snowy Day+	Ezra Jack Keats	Ezra Jack Keats	3	African American
1964	Where the Wild Things Are+	Maurice Sendak	Maurice Sendak	7	
1965	May I Bring a Friend?	Beni Montresor	Beatrice Schenk de Regniers	2	

(continued)

84

Readability levels for Caldecott Medal books (continued)

Award year	Title	Illustrator	Author	Readability level	Cultural focus
1966	*Always Room for One More*	Nonny Hogrogian	Sorche Nic Leodhas, pseud. (Leclaire Alger)	6	Scottish Folktale
1967	*Sam, Bangs, & Moonshine*	Evaline Ness	Evaline Ness	4	
1968	*Drummer Hoff**	Ed Emberley	Barbara Emberley	7	
1969	*The Fool of the World and the Flying Ship*	Uri Shulevitz	Retold by Arthur Ransome	7	Russian
1970	*Sylvester and the Magic Pebble*	William Steig	William Steig	6	
1971	*A Story A Story*	Gail E. Haley	Retold by Gail E. Haley	6	African
1972	*One Fine Day*	Nonny Hogrogian	Retold by Nonny Hogrogian	6	
1973	*The Funny Little Woman*	Blair Lent	Retold by Arlene Mosel	5	Japanese
1974	*Duffy and the Devil*	Margot Zemach	Retold by Harve Zemach	5	Cornish Tale
1975	*Arrow to the Sun +*	Gerald McDermott	Gerald McDermott	3	Pueblo Indian Tale
1976	*Why Mosquitoes Buzz in People's Ears*	Leo & Diane Dillon	Retold by Verna Aardema	5	West Tale
1977	*Ashanti to Zulu: African Traditions*	Leo & Diane Dillion	Margaret Musgrove	6	African Traditions
1978	*Noah's Ark**	Peter Spier	Peter Spier	3	
1979	*The Girl Who Loved Wild Horses*	Paul Goble	Paul Goble	5	Native American
1980	*Ox-Cart Man*	Barbara Cooney	Donald Hall	5	
1981	*Fables*	Arnold Lobel	Arnold Lobel	4	
1982	*Jumanji*	Chris Van Allsburg	Chris Van Allsburg	5	
1983	*Shadow*	Marcia Brown	Blaise Cendrars, trans. by Marcia Brown	4	French
1984	*The Glorious Flight: Across the Channel with Louis Bleriot*	Alice & Martin Provensen	Alice & Martin Provensen	5	
1985	*Saint George and the Dragon*	Trina Schart Hyman	Retold by Margaret Hodges	7	
1986	*The Polar Express*	Chris Van Allsburg	Chris Van Allsburg	3	
1987	*Hey Al*	Richard Egielski	Arthur Yorinks	2	
1988	*Owl Moon*	John Schoenherr	Jane Yolen	4	
1989	*Song and Dance Man*	Stephen Gammell	Karen Ackerman	6	
1990	*Lon Po Po: A Red Riding Hood Story from China*	Ed Young	Ed Young	2	Chinese Folktale

(continued)

Readability levels for Caldecott Medal books (continued)

Award year	Title	Illustrator	Author	Readability level	Cultural focus
1991	*Black and White*	David Macaulay	David Macaulay	5	
1992	*Tuesday**	David Wiesner	David Wiesner	0	
1993	*Mirette on the High Wire*	Emily Arnold McCully	Emily Arnold McCully	4	French
1994	*Grandfather's Journey*	Allen Say	Allen Say, edited by Walter Lorraine	6	Japanese
1995	*Smoky Night*	David Diaz	Eve Bunting	2	African American
1996	*Officer Buckle and Gloria*	Peggy Rathmann	Peggy Rathmann	7	
1997	*Golem*	David Wisniewski	David Wisniewski	6	Jewish legend
1998	*Rapunzel*	Paul O. Zelinsky	Paul O. Zelinsky	6	German fairy tale

* Denotes books with fewer than 200 words
\+ Denotes books with 200–399 words

ninth-grade reading levels, although a great many of the books are so full of humor and imagination that they are a delight even for adults.

Implications and suggestions

The list of Caldecott books forms an excellent source for teachers and parents of younger children seeking appealing and interesting reading material. Further, though the Caldecott Medal is for illustration, many of the award books have great literary as well as artistic merit. Notable among those appropriate for early grades are such works as *Smoky Night* by Eve Bunting, with a second-grade readability level, and *The Polar Express* by Chris Van Allsburg and *The Snowy Day* by Ezra Jack Keats, both with a third-grade readability level. All of these stories are well written and so memorable that they can be convincingly retold without pictures. And even *Tuesday*, with its mere 18 words, forms a charming story that people of any age can interpret and enjoy.

In today's classroom, where multicultural studies are increasingly emphasized, the Caldecotts offer a rich list of cultural stories, fables, and folktales, as indicated under the cultural focus heading in the Table. Many of the books, from 1939's *Mei Li* to 1998's retelling of *Rapunzel*, cover a wide range of cultures including Russian, African, Japanese, Indian, and Native American. Representing almost 40% of the Caldecott books, this multicultural group has an average readability of Grade 5, and the style of the illustrations often provides a second level of cultural information that can effectively complement and augment the text.

Although the Caldecott Medal recognizes picture storybooks, the literary content of many, if not most, of the award winners is strong enough to provide excellent reading material for all elementary-level students. Some suggestions for the classroom use of Caldecott books are described below.

Resource list. Keep this list of readability levels on your desk as a resource to help guide students in choosing appropriate books in their areas of interest and ability.

Read-alouds. Read aloud good Caldecott books whose reading level goes beyond the students' own reading ability. This will help to expose students to new vocabulary and a wide assortment of topics.

Thematic studies. Use a good Caldecott as a springboard for thematic studies or simply to model a love of reading. For example, after reading and discussing Ezra Jack Keats's *The Snowy Day*, read more of his books and encourage discussion of similarities and differences in the illustrations, individual students' preference of one story over another, or ways in which the stories vary.

Extension activities. Encourage children to echo (not copy) the ideas in a book such as Sendak's *Where the Wild Things Are*. For example, children could use the illustrations as a base for creating their own "Wild Thing," such as a hand puppet, a model, or a drawing, that could illustrate a story to go along with the new "Thing." Excellent sources for the further imaginative use of Caldecott books in the classroom are books such as Christine Boardman Moen's *Teaching With Caldecott Books* (1991) and Joan Novelli's *Using Caldecotts Across the Curriculum* (1998).

Discussion groups. Encourage student discussions based on a shared Caldecott book. Even young students can evaluate the reality or imaginative qualities of the story the character traits illustrated, or the ways in which the main character handles the situation shown.

The Caldecott Medal books provide a first-rate combination of appeal to student interest and range of readability levels, encompassing prereaders' read-aloud books through elementary school levels. Using the readability-level charts provided here, teachers can help ensure that their students have a successful engagement with high-quality and interesting books that are at an appropriate reading level. Enjoyable, high-quality reading experiences are the cornerstone for the enjoyment of learning throughout life.

REFERENCES

Association for Library Service to Children. (1995). *The Newbery and Caldecott Awards*. Chicago: American Library Association.

Fry, E. (1977). Fry's readability graph: Clarifications, validity and extensions to level 17. *Journal of Reading, 21*, 242–252.

Leal, D.J., & Chamberlain-Solecki, J. (1998). A Newbery Medal-winning combination: High student interest plus appropriate readability levels. *The Reading Teacher, 51,* 712–714.

Moen, C.B. (1991). *Teaching with Caldecott books.* New York: Scholastic Professional Books.

Novelli, J. (1998). *Using Caldecotts across the curriculum.* New York: Scholastic Professional Books.

Shafritz, J.M., Koeppe, R.P., & Soper, E.W. (1988). *The Facts On File dictionary of education.* New York: Facts on File.

A Newbery Medal-winning combination: High student interest plus appropriate readability levels

Dorothy J. Leal
Julia Chamberlain-Solecki

Volume 51, Number 8, May 1998

There has been an explosion of interest in children's award-winning literature in the last decade. With the escalating interest in literature-based learning, prestigious awards such as the Newbery and Caldecott are becoming even more prized. Topics and genres for these award books are multifaceted, and there are books to meet most students' interests. Yet teachers still wonder how to help students select good books that match their interests while at the same time provide a comfortable readability level.

Newbery Medal books quite easily engage students' interests. However, finding Newbery books that match an individual student's ability level can be a challenge. In order to provide information about readability levels, we examine each Newbery award-winning title from 1922 to 1997.

The readability level of a book is an important consideration for evaluating age-level reading appropriateness. The term *readability* refers to "the level of difficulty of the content, vocabulary, and structure" (Shafritz, Koeppe, & Soper, 1988, p. 385). The focus for our study of Newbery Medal books is on the level of difficulty.

The Fry readability formula, selected for this study, is based on the average of the (a) number of sentences in three 100-word passages and (b) number of syllables in three 100-word passages (Fry, 1977). The average of the three passages for both number of sentences and number of syllables is then charted on the Fry graph to determine grade-level readability. We randomly selected passages to evaluate at the beginning, middle, and end of each of the books.

Readability outcomes can vary greatly because of the passages selected. For instance, if a passage with conversation is selected, the readability level often is lower than for a descriptive passage. Or, in the case of the 1989 award winner, *Joyful*

Noise, levels ranged from Grades 1 to 11 because there were entire poems without any punctuation to indicate sentence length. For this reason, we also report the range of levels found for the three passages.

Some interesting findings

Once the individual readability level was established for each book, computations were done to determine an average grade level for all books over the 76 years of awards. Interestingly, the overall grade-level average for all Newbery books is 6.8. Grade-level findings for each of the 76 Newbery Medal books are reported in the Table. In addition, when examining the books for the highest grade-level ratings, we found that 6% of all award books had a 9th to 10th grade readability grade level. These books may therefore exceed the 14-year-old limit specified in the Newbery criteria. These criteria state that the award is for children, and that "'Children' are defined as persons of ages up to and including fourteen, and books for this entire age range are to be considered" (Association for Library Service to Children, 1995, p. 3). In contrast, when examining books for the lowest grade-level ratings, we found nine books, 13% of all Newbery award winners, with a fourth to fifth grade readability level. It was most surprising to find that there were no award books with a readability level below fourth grade, that is, for readers under 9 to 10 years old. Indeed, only one book, *Shiloh* by Phyllis Naylor, was rated at the fourth-grade level.

Suggestions for the future

If teachers, parents, and older students are seeking to find and honor excellent books, then the Newbery books are an excellent choice. It is clear, however, that Newbery Medal books are not meant for independent reading by younger children. Some excellent Caldecott medal books have wonderful stories that could receive literary awards as well as artistic ones. For instance, *Smoky* Night by Eve Bunting, with a second-grade readability level, and *The Polar Express* by Chris VanAllsburg, with a low third-grade readability level, are both examples of well-written stories for younger children. In fact, these stories are so memorable that they can be convincingly retold without pictures. Yet the Caldecott awards have typically been given to books for younger children and are based primarily on artistic quality. Perhaps it is time for the Newbery criteria to be reworked to include at least two awards based on age-appropriate standards. To select only one book to award for literary excellence for all children up to age 14 is no longer sufficient or reflective of today's cultural and educational needs of children. Many well-crafted children's books are published each year for younger children as well.

This study reveals that up until now the award has recognized excellent literature for children ages 9 to 16. We recommend that a separate category, targeting younger children, be established for recognizing the literary quality of books for emergent readers. Perhaps establishing a Newbery Medal with criteria specific to

Readability levels for Newbery Medal books

Year	Title	Author	Readability grade level	Readability grade range
1922	*The Story of Mankind*	Hendrik W. VanLoon	10	7–16
1923	*The Voyages of Doctor Dolittle*	Hugh Lofting	8	6–10
1924	*The Dark Frigate*	Charles Hawes	8	7–9
1925	*Tales From Silver Lands*	Charles Finger	8	8–9
1926	*Shen of the Sea*	Arthur B. Chrisman	6	4–6
1927	*Smoky, the Cowhorse*	Will James	9	8–9
1928	*Gayneck, the Story of a Pigeon*	Dhan Gopal Mukerji	7	6–7
1929	*The Trumpeter of Krakow*	Eric P. Kelly	8	7–9
1930	*Hitty, Her First Hundred Years*	Rachel Field	8	7–9
1931	*The Cat Who Went to Heaven*	Elizabeth Coatsworth	7	6–9
1932	*Waterless Mountain*	Laura Adams Armer	7	6–8
1933	*Young Fu of the Upper Yangtze*	Elizabeth F. Lewis	7	4–9
1934	*Invincible Louisa: The Story of the Author of Little Women*	Cornelia Meigs	8	8–9
1935	*Dobry*	Monica Shannon	8	7–9
1936	*Caddie Woodlawn*	Carol Ryrie Brink	7	6–9
1937	*Roller Skates*	Ruth Sawyer	6	5–8
1938	*The White Stag*	Kate Seredy	7	7–8
1939	*Thimble Summer*	Elizabeth Enright	6	6–7
1940	*Daniel Boone*	James Daugherty	8	8–9
1941	*Call It Courage*	Armstrong Sperry	7	6–7
1942	*The Matchlock Gun*	Walter D. Edmonds	6	4–7
1943	*Adam of the Road*	Elizabeth Janet Gray	8	7–9
1944	*Johnny Tremain*	Esther Forbes	6	6–7
1945	*Rabbit Hill*	Robert Lawson	9	8–11
1946	*Strawberry Girl*	Lois Lenski	5	4–6
1947	*Miss Hickory*	Carolyn S. Bailey	7	6–7
1948	*The Twenty-One Balloons*	William Pene du Bois	8	7–11
1949	*King of the Wind*	Marguerite Henry	7	7
1950	*The Door in the Wall*	Marguerite de Angeli	5	4–6
1951	*Amos Fortune, Free Man*	Elizabeth Yates	7	4–9
1952	*Ginger Pye*	Eleanor Estes	7	4–8
1953	*Secret of the Andes*	Ann Nolan Clark	6	4–7
1954	*...And Now Miguel*	Joseph Krumgold	6	5–7
1955	*The Wheel on the School*	Meindert DeJong	5	3–7
1956	*Carry On, Mr. Bowditch*	Jean Lee Latham	5	4–7
1957	*Miracles on Maple Hill*	Virginia Sorenson	6	5–9
1958	*Rifles for Watie*	Harold Keith	6	4–6
1959	*The Witch of Blackbird Pond*	Elizabeth George Speare	7	6–8
1960	*Onion John*	Joseph Krumgold	6	5–7
1961	*Island of the Blue Dolphins*	Scott O'Dell	5	3–6

(continued)

Readability levels for Newbery Medal books (continued)

Year	Title	Author	Readability grade level	Readability grade range
1962	*The Bronze Bow*	Elizabeth G. Speare	6	4–7
1963	*A Wrinkle in Time*	Madeline L'Engle	6	3–8
1964	*It's Like This, Cat*	Emily Cheney Neville	7	7–8
1965	*Shadow of a Bull*	Maia Wojciechowska	7	6–8
1966	*I, Juan de Pareja*	Elizabeth B. de Trevino	7	6–9
1967	*Up a Road Slowly*	Irene Hunt	9	8–12
1968	*From the Mixed-Up Files of Mrs. Basil E. Frankweiler*	E.L. Konigsburg	6	5–8
1969	*The High King*	Lloyd Alexander	7	5–8
1970	*Sounder*	William H. Armstrong	7	6–8
1971	*Summer of the Swans*	Betsy Byars	7	6–9
1972	*Mrs. Frisby and the Rats of NIMH*	Robert C. O'Brien	7	6–8
1973	*Julie of the Wolves*	Jean Craighead George	6	5–7
1974	*The Slave Dancer*	Paula Fox	7	3–9
1975	*M.C. Higgins, the Great*	Virginia Hamilton	6	5–6
1976	*The Grey King*	Susan Cooper	7	6–8
1977	*Roll of Thunder, Hear My Cry*	Mildred D. Taylor	8	8
1978	*Bridge to Terabithia*	Katherine Paterson	6	3–6
1979	*The Westing Game*	Ellen Raskin	7	7–8
1980	*A Gathering of Days: A New England Girl's Journal, 1830–1832*	Joan W. Blos	7	4–8
1981	*Jacob Have I Loved*	Katherine Paterson	8	7–8
1982	*A Visit to William Blake's Inn: Poems for Innocent and Experienced Travelers*	Nancy Willard	6	5–7
1983	*Dicey's Song*	Cynthia Voigt	7	7
1984	*Dear Mr. Henshaw*	Beverly Cleary	5	4–10
1985	*The Hero and the Crown*	Robin McKinley	8	8
1986	*Sarah, Plain and Tall*	Patricia MacLachlan	5	3–6
1987	*The Whipping Boy*	Sid Fleischman	5	4–6
1988	*Lincoln: A Photobiography*	Russell Freedman	9	9–10
1989	*Joyful Noise: Poems for Two Voices*	Paul Fleischman	5	1–11
1990	*Number the Stars*	Lois Lowry	8	7–10
1991	*Maniac Magee*	Jerry Spinelli	6	5–7
1992	*Shiloh*	Phyllis R. Naylor	4	3–7
1993	*Missing May*	Cynthia Rylant	7	7
1994	*The Giver*	Lois Lowry	7	7
1995	*Walk Two Moons*	Sharon Creech	6	4–7
1996	*The Midwife's Apprentice*	Karen Cushman	7	6–9
1997	*The View from Saturday*	E.L. Konigsburg	7	6–9

this age would encourage the writing of more quality books for younger children and emergent readers.

Newberys in the classroom

More and more teachers are using Newbery-winning books in their classrooms. Here are some ways Newbery books can be a part of elementary classrooms.

- *Resource list*. Keep this list of readability levels and ranges on your desk as a resource to help guide students in choosing appropriate books in their areas of interest. Inviting each student to fill out an interest inventory provides the teacher with an excellent way to match specific books to children's individual interests with an appropriate reading level. In addition, you can make this list available for your students' personal use, encouraging them to create a personalized Newbery reading list on specific topics.

- *Read-alouds*. Read aloud Newbery books that are beyond the students' own reading ability to broaden student exposure to new vocabulary while increasing student knowledge of both topic and text structure. Classes and students who read and discuss books together often find themselves part of an exciting reading community that extends to creating book projects together.

- *Thematic studies*. Use a Newbery book as a springboard for thematic studies or simply to model a love of reading. Newberys on similar topics can be studied with classroom units. For instance, diverse books dealing with discrimination such as Yates's *Amos Fortune, Free Man* and Cushman's *The Midwife's Apprentice* can be read and compared to understand the underlying issues. In addition, books with similar themes, similar periods in history, or similar geographic locations can be read and examined. Comparing and contrasting similar writing styles would be an appropriate activity for older students.

- *Discussion groups*. Encourage Newbery discussion groups in the class. Gambrell and Almasi's book *Lively Discussions! Fostering Engaged Reading* (1996) is one source with many suggestions for encouraging student discussions and creating a warm reading climate in the classroom.

- *Newbery clubs*. Create a Newbery club where students choose different Newbery books to read and then come together with students from other classes to share thoughts and ideas about the theme or contents. One exciting way to give students ownership of the club is to make them responsible for reading, reviewing, and ranking the books according to their own preferences. A large student-generated wall chart could be developed for the school library to track student recommendations of appropriate audiences for each book read and personal evaluations of the best of the Newbery books.

• *Mock Newbery elections*. Give students responsibility for passing judgment on the Newberys. One enjoyable activity is to have a mock Newbery evaluation trial. Here different groups of students read and evaluate a set of Newbery books. Either the American Library Association criteria or student-generated criteria can be the basis for reading, then ranking the books, and finally building a strong defense for their choices. This defense is then presented in a group setting. Following the presentation and some lively discussions, the class then votes to decide which book gets the award and which books are honor books.

REFERENCES

Association for Library Service to Children. (1995). *The Newbery and Caldecott awards*. Chicago: American Library Association.

Fry, E. (1977). Fry's readability graph: Clarifications, validity and extension to level 17. *Journal of Reading, 21*, 242–252.

Gambrell, L.B., & Almasi, J.F. (1996). *Lively discussions! Fostering engaged reading*. Newark, DE: International Reading Association.

Shafritz, J.M., Koeppe, R.P., & Soper, E.W. (1988). *The Facts On File dictionary of education*. New York: Facts On File.

Should we travel by plane, car, train, or bus? Teacher/child collaboration in developing a thematic literacy center

Carolyn Ann Walker
Donna Allen
Debbie Glines

VOLUME 50, NUMBER 6, MARCH 1997

Children have opportunities to increase their understanding of the forms and functions of literacy by participating in thematic reading and writing activities in dramatic play contexts (Christie, 1991; Pellegrini & Galda, 1993; Vukelich, 1994; Walker, 1994). This type of thematic play provides opportunities for children to use multiple forms of literacy in a variety of ways.

Teachers are sometimes encouraged to guide the development and implementation of these types of thematic centers by initiating and developing themes, by selecting literacy materials, and by modeling literacy behaviors during play (Christie, 1991; Vukelich, 1994). While this type of assistance certainly appears helpful, such approaches may be rejected by children (Walker, 1991) or may lessen their ownership of reading and writing in thematic play contexts.

Perhaps a better model of assisting children can be found by examining children's out-of-school literacy activities. Many of these activities are initiated by children and are focused on the child's needs or interests. For example, children who participate in book sharing at home often have a say in the book selection, the setting in which it is read, and the duration of the reading. If this collaborative model were applied to the development of thematic literacy activities in play contexts, children might have more control. In this article, we describe our attempts to collaborate with preschool children in the development of themed reading and writing activities in a travel agency play center in our classroom.

Collaboration rather than prescription

Debbie and Donna's preschool classroom is a busy place with a variety of activities going on. The children come to school on Tuesday and Thursday mornings. We provide a variety of activities and centers in the room, including reading, art/easel, listening, sand/water, computer, kitchen, dress up, blocks, table toys, and writing. Free play occurs during each class session, and children are allowed to move around the centers in the classroom (including the travel agency center).

The thematic play center described in this article is the product of the shared decision making of teachers and children. We wanted the children to have a say in the selection of the topic for the center. We were also interested in including more reading and writing opportunities for the children. We wanted the children's play to be focused around a central theme so that their use of literacy would be connected and would serve many functions in the context of the theme.

Before we selected literacy materials and developed the writing center, we gave the children an opportunity to chose a topic that interested them. We introduced several theme choices during circle time. The travel agency was included as a choice because the children expressed interest in and experience with travel during a transportation unit, and because there were multiple opportunities for children to engage in reading and writing within this theme. We asked the children to vote for their favorite theme, and they unanimously selected the travel agency.

Next, we gathered a variety of literacy materials that reflected the theme of the travel agency. These included an adding machine, a stamp pad with dates, paper, markers and pencils, maps, travel brochures, a preprinted travel plan form, and a phone book. A local travel agency donated brochures that featured Disney World. We placed these materials along with other items such as tables and chairs in an arrangement that approximated a travel agency. Forms, brochures, and supplies such as the phone book were visible and available for the children to use.

Only the travel form (see Figure 1) was formally introduced to the children. We discussed its content and uses during circle time so that the children would know what the form was for and how it could be used. The form addressed the major elements of travel and a travel agency. It included a space for the name of the child who was traveling, a space to indicate where the child/children wanted to go, pictures of the mode of transportation and accommodations, and pictures of meals from which to choose. There was also a signature line for the travel agent.

The children began using the travel agency as soon as it was ready. They were allowed to come and go as they chose, and other than the explanation of the travel form our participation in the literacy activities and other aspects of the play was limited to questions asked of us by the children. We formally and informally observed the children's thematic play for the

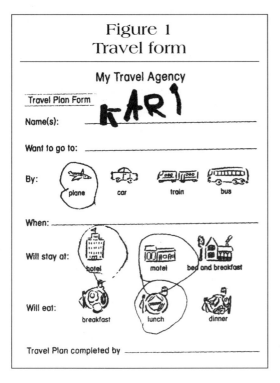

Figure 1
Travel form

My Travel Agency

Travel Plan Form

Name(s): **KARI**

Want to go to: _____

By: plane   car   train   bus

When: _____

Will stay at: hotel   motel   bed and breakfast

Will eat: breakfast   lunch   dinner

Travel Plan completed by _____

2 months that the travel agency was in the room. One teacher conducted six formal observations during the free 30-minute play period on separate days. These observations included note taking that described the children's actions and dialogue. Both teachers also informally observed the children throughout the 2 months that the center was used. Samples of the children's writing were collected. Throughout the period that the children were observed, and afterward, the data gathered were examined for themes relating to the use of literacy in the travel agency.

Literacy in the travel agency

The children viewed literacy as an integral part of the travel agency, and they explored its many functions and uses. They integrated reading and writing into their play activities as they planned trips and made reservations. This integration was similar to real life integration of reading and writing in a travel agency context. As the children prepared to take trips and planned trips for others they looked at and "read" brochures; looked up phone numbers; and made phone calls, plane reservations, and arrangements for hotels and restaurants. They used emergent writing to convey information as they filled out travel forms. The children also represented other real life literacy uses that related to trip planning. In addition to writing information about trip planning, they made lists for trips and wrote postcards to send back while they were on vacation. These findings support Halliday's (1978) description of young children's language as complex and multifunctional, as well as Teale & Sulzby's (1986) descriptions of literacy development as emerging and functionally based.

Literacy also served the function of bringing and keeping children together within a number of literacy-focused play activities. Because there were no set limits by the teachers as to who could participate in the travel agency at a given time, the children often included friends in their play. Without being told, they assigned roles, selected play partners, and related their behaviors to the topic of the travel agency. This supports Rogoff's (1990) explanation of the importance of peer interaction in play and the potential for children to scaffold one another's learning. Just as Rogoff concluded, these children had both the time and interest to help one another.

Making plans with literacy-related materials

An important benefit of the travel agency was that it seemed to help the children become more comfortable engaging in emergent writing. The travel agency was a popular place for the children to write. During other activities they seemed to be concerned about spelling words correctly, but in the travel agency center they wrote freely and focused on the functional uses of the print rather than spelling. We were somewhat surprised that they were so much more interested in and willing to participate in this writing rather than in other classroom writing projects. Perhaps it was because they were able to choose their topic rather than be assigned a theme topic from the teacher.

The children who played in the travel agency not only engaged more willingly in writing but also understood that the written symbols they created and read conveyed meaning. They understood that information needed to be recorded in written form, and they did this while preparing forms and tickets. Further, the children used literacy materials during play for purposes that approximated nonplay uses. Writing samples support this finding and

indicate that while the children's emergent writing varied, they wrote the letters of their names on the forms and sometimes wrote other letter strings for sections of the forms such as where the traveler was to go (see Figure 2).

Figure 2
Children's emergent writing samples

Developing a successful collaboration

The children in our classroom really enjoyed playing in the travel agency. Some months later they were still asking us to get the materials out (including the literacy materials) and revive this center. Several factors seemed to work together to make this experience such a success. These include the children's experience with the theme topic, the instructional focus on travel and literacy activities related to travel outside of their immediate context, and the children's input in decision making about the theme choice. We suggest several guidelines based on these factors for teachers interested in the development of a literacy-focused thematic center.

• *Determine the experience base of your students*. We found that a number of the children had background experience with travel. Many of them had taken trips and understood the basic concepts of travel, so their play was essentially a familiar context. This familiarity was valuable for the children because it provided them an opportunity to revisit forms and functions of reading and writing.

Teachers can determine a child's experience with a topic or theme through informal discussion or through more formal surveys of experience. We asked the children about their experiences with travel. Parents also have knowledge of their family experiences.

This approach may not be sufficient in all circumstances, however. Another approach for gaining information about children's experiences is by using a literacy experience or functions of print inventory such as the one developed by Weiss and Hagen (1988). This type of inventory can be individualized according to curriculum goals or a student's experiences. For example, you may want to ask the following broad response questions or statements: "What types of reading and writing do you and your family do?" "Tell me some of the places where you have seen people reading and/or writing outside of your home," and "Do you know why you or others in your family (or the people outside of your home) were reading or writing?" As you gain information about your students' experiences you will be able to more fully determine the benefits or potential drawbacks of literacy-focused themes for play.

• *Provide choices for your students and honor their decisions*. Our students selected the travel agency topic from a number of suggestions that we provided. The success of this approach is evident in the children's consistent interest in literacy activities in the travel agency. Teachers might even want to consider extending this approach to further encourage a child-centered approach. It might be appropriate to have children generate lists of their interests from which themes can be selected.

• *Consider providing theme-based literacy modeling outside of the play context either as part of a larger unit or through brief yet focused direct instruction*. Our students had opportunities to learn about the forms and functions of literacy from their own experiences and from brief yet focused direct instruction outside of the context of play. During circle time we presented the travel form to the children by explaining how the form could be used and what the pictures and spaces on the form were for. This approach provided a way for the children to participate in a focused discussion of the uses of one type of literacy material and gave us some assurance that the children understood its uses. This approach did not intervene directly into the children's play, however, and left the children's literacy choices and behaviors during play as child initiated. This perspective is congruent with views of children as active initiators and participants in their literacy learning (Strickland & Morrow, 1989; Teale & Sulzby, 1986).

Teachers and children can also work together to select and obtain literacy-related materials for thematic centers. During field trips to various stores or agencies teachers and children can request literacy-related items. Children can discuss whether or not they feel items are appropriate and how to make or obtain other items.

Another approach for helping children understand literacy activities and materials is to model the types of reading and writing that will occur. For example, if you are studying community helpers such as postal workers, then it is appropriate to show the children what a postal worker does, including reading, sorting, weighing, and delivering mail. In this way children will develop understanding in a contextual manner.

It was not difficult to develop the travel agency play center. It simply required that we be familiar with and have an understanding of our children's background experiences and that we have a desire to continue to build those experiences. We used materials from home and school, and we were also given materials from businesses.

In our case, the benefits of this process included sustained child interest and participation in the literacy activities in the center. We encourage all teachers to consider collaborating with children in the development of thematic literacy activities in play contexts. We were very pleased with our collaboration. You, like us, might be amazed at how involved children can get when the idea comes from them!

REFERENCES

Christie, J.F. (1991). Play and early literacy development: Summary and discussion. In J.F. Christie (Ed.), *Play and early literacy development* (pp. 233–246). New York: State University of New York Press.

Halliday, M.A.K. (1978). *Language as social semiotic*. London: University Park Press.

Pellegrini, A.D., & Galda, L. (1993). Ten years after: A reexamination of symbolic play and literacy research. *Reading Research Quarterly, 28,* 165–175.

Rogoff, B. (1990). *Apprenticeship in thinking: Conceiving development in social context.* New York: Oxford University Press.

Strickland, D., & Morrow, L. (Eds.). (1989). *Emerging literacy: Young children learn to read and write.* Newark, DE: International Reading Association.

Teale, W., & Sulzby, E. (Eds.). (1986). *Emergent literacy: Writing and reading.* Norwood, NJ: Ablex.

Vukelich, C. (1994). Effects of play interventions on young children's reading of environmental print. *Early Childhood Research Quarterly, 9,* 153–170.

Walker, C. (1991). *Dramatic play and literacy centers.* Unpublished data.

Walker, C. (1994). *Contexts for literacy development: A study of literacy practices during dramatic play in one Head Start classroom.* Unpublished doctoral dissertation, Purdue University, West Lafayette, IN.

Weiss, M., & Hagen, R. (1988). A key to literacy: Kindergartners' awareness of the functions of print. *The Reading Teacher, 41,* 575–578.

Emerging literacy: Message boards in preschool

Barbara Laster
Betty Conte

VOLUME 52, NUMBER 4, DECEMBER 1998/JANUARY 1999

Four-year-old Tanya (all children's names are pseudonyms) wrote a message to me on our refrigerator notepad, "I LOVE YOU!!!" In many homes, the refrigerator message board or the pad next to the telephone is a place for important communication. The messages are spontaneous and natural. They are aimed at a specific audience. And, most important, they are authentically meaningful. Some of the communication occurs with text, and some is pictorial. Anna, Josh, Chris, Juan, Rose, Andy, and Mohammed, all 4-year-olds in a public prekindergarten program, wrote in a similar way in their classroom.

What is it?

The Message Board activity is a voluntary sharing of important events or messages on large or student-sized chalkboards. Whereas journals are private, Message Boards are public and are used by some students, parents, and teachers every day. There are three stages of learning. First, the teacher models the pictowriting for authentic communication. Second, student-initiated writing is encouraged and supported. Third, verbal sharing among all students in the classroom enhances the social aspects of language development and emergent literacy.

Teacher modeling

At the beginning and throughout the year, the teacher models writing for authentic purposes. Every day, the teacher writes and/or draws information that is current and meaningful on the top half of the chalkboard. For example, the teacher might inform the children of a change in routine or that one child has a special celebration. The teacher might write or draw to remind students to do something, such as take their art projects home. On one particular day, Ms. Conte drew a message to help students remember to stay on the path when they walked to the playground; another day she shared news about the class pet (see Figure 1).

Figure 1
An example of a daily Message Board

Messages
1. Teacher's—"Izzy [the pet iguana] is going to Mrs. Cushman's class."
2. Anthony—"One day, after school, in five weeks, when it's daytime I'm going to play tee ball."
3. Van—"I was happy because I got a tattoo from my daddy."
4. Katya—"I got new shoes."
5. Derek—"This is my Dad, my Mom, me, my sister, and my friend Jessica. I'm going to her house today."

Encouraging student pictowriting

Students draw pictures and write text about important events in their lives on the bottom half of the chalkboard. This is a voluntary activity, and some students feel comfortable writing or drawing during the first week of school. The teacher, though, can often prompt students as to what would make a good message. For example, a child might make a special creation in the block corner or art center, and the teacher may suggest that he or she share it by writing it on the Message Board. If the teacher sees a reluctant writer, she may in-vite the child to share news from his or her family, such as the child's response to a special celebration or a new baby. Ms. Conte noticed one morning that Juan had made a beautiful bead necklace in the art corner. Although he had not yet written on the Message Board, with Ms. Conte's encouragement, Juan wrote his first message: a picture of his bead necklace and the letter *J*.

Talking about personal messages

The essential third part of the activity is the verbal exchange that creates a learning community. On the basis of their written messages, students have the opportunity to share orally with the class. Exchanges about the message are conversational and unpressured. Early one morning, Andy drew three buildings, and with assistance solicited from Ms. Conte he wrote a word. He told the class: "This is me. I went to my cousin's house. Then I went to Publix and to church. That is why I didn't come to school." Almost every day, Andy had another message that included some alphanumeric symbols.

The child who is listening is learning just as much as the student who is writing and speaking. Questions by peers and teachers often extend the conversation as concepts are discussed. Especially at the beginning of the school year, a teacher may help extend the message by describing what has been drawn or by asking open-ended questions. For example, the teacher may invite a student to tell about where, when, and how an event happened that is portrayed in a student message. The teacher is a facilitator rather than a director of this verbal process; thus, the teacher remains part of the group by being a colearner with the children.

Sometimes children tell about their messages in a language other than the one dominating the classroom. For example, in Ms. Conte's classroom, Anna spoke in Spanish for the first 3 months after her arrival from South America. Teacher support took the form of translation. This gave Anna the opportunity to know that she was really communicating with her peers and that she was a valued member of the community. Subsequently, for several weeks Anna used some English words mixed with Spanish. As time passed, she chose to speak English so that her peers could understand her message without translation.

How to do it

An appropriate time to begin the Message Board activity is as the children enter the classroom. It is a natural bridge between home life and school learning. When the children walk in and are greeted by the teacher, one activity they can choose is to write or draw on the Message Board. On a typical day in Ms. Conte's classroom, at 8:15 a.m., four to six children are drawing/writing their messages across the bottom half of the large chalkboard. Three children are seated on the rug and are using small chalkboards for the same purpose. Clusters of other children are doing puzzles, using the stamp pads or dough, building with blocks, or talking quietly. Messages stay on the chalkboard all day, and children or adults add to the Message Board throughout the day.

These messages are the impetus for the class discussion that has replaced "circle time" or "greeting time." Everyone who writes gets a turn to share. Sometimes the sharing of messages must occur at more than one session because there have been so many messages or such extensive discussion. When there are too many messages to be shared in one session, the teacher will draw a line to delineate messages that will be shared later in the day at another large-group time. (In September, sharing time is typically 10 minutes; by March, 20 minutes is often needed to allow everyone time to share.) Messages are often used at the end of the day by the teacher to facilitate planning for the next day's lesson or as a means of remembering significant anecdotes for assessment purposes.

A variation on rug time

"In traditional Show and Tell, too often children become competitive about the objects that they bring to school," a preschool teacher observed. How do we allow all children to share, yet emphasize the communication rather than the possessions? In the Message Board daily activity, the ideas and events that shape the children beyond the classroom are emphasized. This is done without the stress that often accompanies bringing tangible possessions to greeting time. The Message Board activity is also more student initiated and directly linked to emergent literacy behaviors. It is similar to "rug time" (Cochran-Smith, 1996), in that the needs of individual students are supported while all students are expected to follow certain norms of behavior. Yet the Message Board activity is distinct from rug time in that it emphasizes active, authentic, student-centered literacy rather than passive storybook reading.

Social interaction

Language provides the keys that unlock new social strategies for children. Bredekamp and Copple (1997) say "new social strategies are learned as children listen to others representing their thoughts and feelings" (p. 109). Furthermore, children can learn appropriate strategies for solving problems that involve social interaction. For example, Josh's message told others that he wanted to play with Rose and that Rose rebuffed him. When he shared his message, the teacher directed the conversation so she could guide children to consider appropriate ways to communicate with their peers about their needs.

Language development

The beginning of literacy is language development, communicating meaningful messages. "Providing opportunities for children to talk, carefully listening to children, and offering well-placed expansions of their sentences to enhance the meaning are the most important ways teachers can assist these young language learners" (Bredekamp & Copple, 1997, p. 109). We want to encourage children to become more active participants in language learning (Bredekamp & Copple, 1997; Hohmann & Weikart, 1995). One of the early skills that Message Boards facilitate is recognition of the relationship between written symbols and spoken words. This is an essential first step in learning to read (Beck & Juel, 1992).

A hidden agenda: Guiding emergent literacy

Unconventional ways of using text (miscues) are very helpful for a teacher planning a lesson based on the needs of the children. For example, if after several months of school several children are writing English words right to left, the teacher may give direct instruction to aid students in learning left to right English orthography.

As the year progresses, students feel comfortable adding to their messages as they think of new aspects of their original thoughts during the day. Thus, they are beginning to experience the revision component of the writing process.

A developmental process

In September, most 4-year-olds create messages that are mostly drawn lines on the Message Board. Yet, they invariably have a story (whether real or imaginary) to accompany their pictowriting and are proud to share the meaning in oral communication with the class. After a few weeks, most children choose to identify their messages with some text writing. In the first stage, children write their names or parts of their names; later they write text for the stories that are represented in their pictures on the Message Board.

By October or November, Chris, Juan, and Josh each wrote messages including one another's names. They drew arrows toward one another's messages to indicate who would call whom about their plans concerning the upcoming youth fair because they wanted to attend it together.

In May, Rose wrote a number 3 at both the top and at the bottom of her elaborate drawing of the first communion celebration that was anticipated for her brother. She also wrote her name and some letters that were the first letters of other important words in the message. She explained to the class: "This is me and my mom and my sister and the first communion of my brother. We are getting ready for it. We are going to sleep 3 days now" (see Figure 2).

Mohammed did not speak any English from September until January. His drawings were immature in that the arms and legs extended from the head with no body. In May, Mohammed shared his first message with the class: three sentences in English about how he had been sick.

From ages 3 to 5, many children are not yet ready to write but can easily draw (Bredekamp & Copple, 1997). There are, of course, individual differences in small motor development; also, many girls tend to advance in this area before boys do. Thus, the preschool classroom should remain unpressured in terms of writing.

Family literacy blurs into classroom literacy

Parents write on the Message Board with the children. Some parents stay to hear the large group discuss messages. One teacher noted that the Message Board activity has encouraged parents, who otherwise would not have done so, to join in the activity of the classroom. Message Boards can also facilitate home-school communication because teachers often learn home information that might otherwise have been missed.

This is me and my Mom and my sister, and the first communion of my brother. We are getting ready for it. We're going to sleep 3 days now.

May 7, 1997

Conclusion

"It is my favorite time of the day," said one teacher about the sharing of the messages. Message Boards is an inviting addition to large-group time in which children expand their thinking, practice their functional communication skills, and develop early reading and writing competencies. Message Boards at school could also have an impact on messages at home. The 4-year-old who wrote on the refrigerator in September took possession of all available self-sticking notes in her home in April and wrote messages all the way up the staircase. Each sticky note had a word or phrase: "Mom" "Dad" "sister" "I love you!" "Tanya."

REFERENCES

Beck, I.L., & Juel, C. (1992). The role of decoding in learning to read. In S.J. Samuels & A.E. Farstrup (Eds.), *What research has to say about reading instruction* (pp. 101–123). Newark, DE: International Reading Association.

Bredekamp, S., & Copple, C. (Eds.). (1997). *Developmentally appropriate practices in early childhood programs serving children from birth through age 8* (Rev. ed.). Washington, DC: National Association for the Education of Young Children.

Cochran-Smith, M. (1996). Rug-time, framework for storyreading: Sitting, listening, and learning new things. In B.M. Power & R.S. Hubbard (Eds.), *Language development: A reader for teachers* (pp. 117–131). Englewood Cliffs, NJ: Prentice Hall.

Hohmann, M., & Weikart, D.P. (1995). *Educating young children*. Ypsilanti, MI: High/Scope Press.

Encouraging young students to use interesting words in their writing

Megan S. Sloan

VOLUME 50, NUMBER 3, NOVEMBER 1996

The difference between the right word and nearly the right word is the same as that between lightning and the lightning bug.

Mark Twain

Good authors use interesting words in their writing. Their language is lively, specific, and beautiful to the ear. This command of vocabulary helps evoke response in readers.

My first-grade and second-grade students are writers. They participate in writers' workshop and follow the steps of the writing process. As beginning writers, they learn to develop their ideas in an organized manner. Still, most students choose ordinary words. They usually write, "It was fun," or "I had a good time."

In my quest to help my students develop into good writers I recognized the need to help them become better stewards of their words.

Sharing literature

I went to the best source for teaching good writing: good books. I share literature full of rich, specific vocabulary (see Figure). We *lunge* into the water like the herons in *In the Small, Small Pond* (Fleming, 1993). We watch the sheep *scatter* through the meadow and the trout *flash* "like jewels in the sunlight" in *All the Places to Love* (MacLachlan, 1994). We smile as Matthew *embraces* Nicoletta in *Matthew's Dream* (Lionni, 1991).

We talk about the interesting words we encounter as I read to the class. My enthusiasm over words sparks word curiosity, resulting in an Interesting Word Wall where our interesting words are posted. Now students look to the wall for new words to try out in their writing.

Minilessons

During minilessons I focus specifically on encouraging the use of interesting words.

Good picture books for teaching about interesting words

Bunting, E. (1994). *Smoky night*. San Diego, CA: Harcourt Brace.
Chute, L. (1988). *Clever Tom and the leprechaun*. New York: Scholastic.
Cohen, C.L. (1988). *The mud pony*. New York: Scholastic.
Cowcher, H. (1991). *Tigress*. New York: Scholastic.
Fox, M. (1988). *Koala lou*. San Diego, CA: Harcourt Brace.
George, W.T. (1989). *Box turtle at long pond*. New York: Trumpet.
Geraghty, P. (1990). *Look out, Patrick*. New York: Trumpet.
Henkes, K. (1991). *Chrysanthemum*. New York: Trumpet.
Mathers, P. (1991). *Sophie and Lou*. New York: Harper Trophy.
McKissack, P. (1988). *Mirandy and brother wind*. New York: Knopf.
Steig, W. (1977). *Caleb and Kate*. New York: Farrar, Straus & Giroux.
Van Allsburg, C. (1988). *Two bad ants*. Boston: Houghton Mifflin.

Interesting word search. Pairs of students look through a book, recording the interesting words they find. Next to the interesting word students write the common word the author could have used.

Act out words. To illustrate the power of words students dramatize several words that differ by shades of meaning (e.g., *sped, raced, crept, tiptoed, sauntered*). The class guesses which word is being portrayed. We put these "word cousins" on a chart for students to use.

Energetic verbs. I read Mem Fox's (1989) *Night Noises* to show a good author's use of lively language. We record the energetic verbs Fox uses to help her story come alive (*rattled, creaked, drummed, drifted, crept*). I encourage students to write like Fox. I read Verna Aardema's (1975) *Why Mosquitoes Buzz in People's Ears*. We find the energetic verbs Aardema uses as each animal is *startled, alarmed, ignored*, and *frightened*. Students act out the story so they can feel the power of different words.

Alphabet books. Some alphabet books are sources for interesting words. My favorite, *Antics* by Cathi Hepworth (1992), is filled with extraordinary words like *jubilant, flamboyant*, and *enchanter*. After reading several ABC books, students pick a theme such as "Animals and Movement" and write their own alphabet book.

Nice-o-nyms. Students brainstorm a list of synonyms for the word *nice*. We post the list in the classroom. We do the same with *said, happy, big*, and other overused words.

Poetry. We talk about the words poets use. Students paint with watercolors while I read the lyrics of Elizabeth Coatsworth, create with clay when I recite Jack Prelutsky's "The Dragons Are Singing Tonight" (1993), and draw cartoons to illustrate Karla Kuskin's "A Bug Sat in a Silver Flower" (1980). I continue to encourage students to give the interesting words life as they recite poems individually or chorally.

As students continue to write, I notice a change. Students replace ordinary words with more interesting ones. Mitch writes, "The cat *pounced* off the piano just as the boy *lunged*." Ben observes "Doug looked a little cross as he *lazily strolled* to the other side of the reeds." Sarah describes how she was "*ostracized*" at her old school.

My focus on words has paid off. Students are writing with a greater command and enjoyment of their language!

Children's books cited

Aardema, V. (1975). *Why mosquitoes buzz in people's ears*. New York: Dutton.

Fleming, D. (1993). *In the small, small pond*. New York: Holt.

Fox, M. (1989). *Night noises*. San Diego, CA: Harcourt Brace.

Hepworth, C. (1992). *Antics*. New York: Trumpet.

Kuskin, K. (1980). A bug sat in a silver flower. In *Dogs & dragons, trees & dreams: A collection of poems* (p. 47). New York: Harper & Row.

Lionni, L. (1991). *Matthew's dream*. New York: Trumpet.

MacLachlan, P. (1994). *All the places to love*. New York: HarperCollins.

Prelutsky, J. (1993). The dragons are singing tonight. In *The dragons are singing tonight* (p. 22). New York: Greenwillow.

The important thing: Connecting reading and writing in the primary grades

Karl A. Matz

Volume 47, Number 1, September 1993

Many teachers, after sharing predictable books with their classes, extend the children's literacy experience by inviting them to write their own versions of the stories. Children enjoy doing so, and the activity can be an effective way to make the reading-writing connection clear and meaningful. For younger children, who may not possess a sophisticated understanding of story structures, many excellent stories are too complex to serve as useful models. Author Margaret Wise Brown's delightful *The Important Book* offers a solution any teacher of the primary grades can implement.

Brown (1949) used a simple pattern in her book. Each page is a self-contained passage featuring a common object. Brown chose one characteristic to be "the important thing," listed several other characteristics of that object, and ended by repeating the important thing, thus:

> The important thing about the sky is
> that it is always there. It is true

> that it is blue and high and full of clouds
> and made of air
> but the important thing about the sky
> is that it is always there.
> (pp. 15–16)

The book, as a whole, is a seemingly random collection of such descriptions. This random organization and simple pattern form a perfect model for young children. Three fun and educationally relevant activities are possible if the teacher has but a single copy of Brown's book.

Choral and repeated reading

The teacher begins, of course, by reading the book to the children. It lends itself especially well to participatory choral reading, since the last line is the same as the first and is always preceded by the word *but*.... Children can easily join in once they've gotten a sense of the pattern.

They begin to listen intently as the first line of each page is read, so as to be ready to recite it when the time comes.

One or more of the descriptive patterns can be written on oaktag and cut into single word cards. Place these in a pocket chart or fasten them to a bulletin board and lead the children in chorally reading the passages until the words are very familiar and can be easily read individually. Then, simply rearrange or scramble the word cards and invite children to reorganize them correctly. The children will find it necessary to identify each word and consider its place in the context of the passage in order to determine its correct location.

A class big book

The class can create its own version of *The Important Book*. Children, as individuals or in pairs, can compose and illustrate a one-page passage based upon the structure appearing in Brown's original. First, invite them to suggest a few objects and descriptive words to complete the sentence pattern "The important thing about a _____ is that it is _____." Provide an example or two, then have the children create some of their own.

The important thing about a bear is that it
is furry.
The important thing about a key is that it
unlocks doors.
The important thing about a peach is that
it is juicy.

After distributing large sheets of paper, the teacher can encourage the children to choose a common object to be the subject of their passage. If necessary, the class can brainstorm a list so that there will be ample subjects from which to choose. Once the subject is chosen, instruct the children to select one characteristic to be the important thing.

Next, have the children write three complete sentences describing other aspects of the item, such as its size, its color, where it is kept, and so forth. Finally, for their closing sentence, direct the children to repeat the first sentence, beginning it with the word *but....*

The important thing about a jar is that it is
clear.
You can put things in it.
It is dangerous when it breaks.
It has a lid that screws on, but...
The important thing about a jar is that it is
clear.

Suggested books for adaptations

Johnson, T. (1988). *Yonder*. New York: Scholastic.
Numeroff, L.J. (1985). *If you give a mouse a cookie*. New York: Scholastic.
Rylant, C. (1982). *When I was young in the mountains*. New York: E.P. Dutton.
Viorst, J. (1972). *Alexander and the terrible, horrible, no good, very bad day*. New York: Aladdin Books.
Viorst, J. (1988). *The good-bye book*. New York: Macmillan.

Due to the random organization of the passages in Brown's text, it is easy to assemble the book in any of several ways without loss of meaning. For example, the teacher may choose to organize the pages alphabetically, creating a dictionary of sorts. Or the pages can be organized according to concepts: animals, foods, plants, and so forth. Regardless of the organization selected, there is no effect upon the book as a whole because each page, while integrated by the pattern, is also complete within itself.

Self-esteem builder

An "important book" can also be written about each child in the class by his or her peers. The process is the same as that which is described above, except that the teacher may wish to use standard-sized paper instead, to form a smaller, more portable book. Each illustrated passage becomes a page in an important book, but, in this case, the personal book is presented to a special child at the end of each week or on some other meaningful day.

One second-grade teacher made each of her weekly "teacher's pets" the subject of a personal important book. Each of her 24 students had his or her own personal important book before the end of the school year. The children enjoyed the routine, it took very little time, and the resulting book became a cherished keepsake and a real self-image builder for its subject.

Adaptations

Children can dictate one-page passages to the teacher, volunteers, or older children acting as cross-age tutors. After the passage is dictated, the children can illustrate their pages and contribute to the class book.

Teachers of older students might encourage more advanced readers and writers to create important books to share with a group of younger children. In this case, the important books can be used to teach concepts or to entertain.

The important thing about dinosaurs is that they are extinct.
They were very big.
Some dinosaurs ate plants and some ate meat.
You can see dinosaur bones in museums.
but
The important thing about dinosaurs is that they are
extinct.

Similar reading-writing connections can be made with other books which have a random organization. *When I Was Young in the Mountains*, by Cynthia Rylant (1982), easily becomes "When We Were Young in the City" or "When We Were Young by the Ocean." Rylant describes her childhood in Appalachia in an almost random assortment of events that provide an easily emulated pattern. *Yonder*, by Tony Johnson (1988), also proves an excellent model but uses the passing of time as an organizational scheme for the otherwise random list of events. Laura Joffe Numeroff's popular *If You Give a*

The important thing Andrea is that she is friendly she is also funny and she is a good swimmer and she is my friend. But the important thing about Andrea is that she is friendly

Tia

TIA

Mouse a Cookie (1985) quickly and easily becomes "If You Give a Car a Wash" or "If You Give Your Friend a Dollar." The cumulative nature of the various events in the story provides a clear model. Judith Viorst's books, being somewhat more complex, are a useful model for older children who have a better understanding of story organization. In particular, *The Good-Bye Book* (1988) and *Alexander and the Terrible, Horrible, No Good, Very Bad Day* (1972) serve as useful models.

The activities described here are easy and inexpensive; they integrate the language arts in authentic, meaningful and very natural ways. Yet, the activities prove to be so engaging and enjoyable that it is easy to overlook the fact that the children are involved in relevant reading and writing, collaborative learning, and the application of planning and organizing skills and strategies.

REFERENCE

Brown, M.W. (1949). *The important book*. New York: Harper Trophy.

Reading and creating counting books

Joan C. Fingon

VOLUME 49, NUMBER 1, SEPTEMBER 1995

Counting books are often used by classroom teachers to help young children become familiar with numbers and sequencing. Older children can learn from counting books that use addition, subtraction, grouping, and other mathematical concepts that extend to sets or higher numbers. Counting books can be simple or elaborate, designed around a particular theme or concept, varied in design and complexity, or appreciated simply for their exquisite illustrations.

Using counting books in the classroom

There are many possibilities for using counting books in the curriculum. One way for students to become familiar with counting books is to have many different types of interesting books available to them for classroom use. With careful planning, teachers can incorporate counting books into their daily routines by using them during story time, or allowing students to select them as a book choice during SSR (Sustained Silent Reading) or

DEAR (Drop Everything And Read) time. The idea of using counting books as an approach during reading time can also be beneficial to students. Students, individually or in groups, might read literature that relates to the concept of the number three. Some choices are *Three Billy Goats Gruff* by Glen Rounds, *The True Story of the Three Little Pigs* by Jon Scieszka, *The Three Little Pigs*, *The Three Sillies*, or *The Three Bears* by Paul Galdone, *Three by Three* by James Krüss, or *The Three Little Hawaiian Pigs and the Magic Shark* by Donivee Laird. Examples of literature for the concept of the number ten include *10 Bears in My Bed; A Goodnight Countdown* by Stan Mack, Russell Hoban's *Ten What? A Mystery Counting Book*, and Judy Viorst's *The Tenth Good Thing About Barney*. Teachers may select counting books based on student interest and reading ability, students could select their own books, or the teacher could prepare a list of books in numerical order according to titles for students to choose from.

Teachers of ESL students might try writing a counting book in a foreign language. Good examples to use in class are Meredith Dunham's *Numbers: How Do You Say It?* which describes and illustrates numbers in French, Spanish, Italian, and English and Muriel Feelings's *Moja Means One: Swahili Counting Book.*

Using counting books in language arts and reading

Many literacy skills can be taught when students write and illustrate their own counting books. Younger students can construct counting books using numbers from one to ten while older students can make books using more complex number concepts such as addition, subtraction, division, sets, or grouping. One interesting way to integrate writing skills through the use of counting books involves students designing their own books based on a number being represented in different ways. Students can work alone on a number or be assigned a series of numbers with a partner. Simple guidelines for instruction could be included. Here is an example for the number five:

5
five, 5%, \$5.00, fifth, V...
$0+5=5, 5+0=5, 1+4=5, 4+1=5, 5+0=5,$
$0+5=5, 2+3=5, 3+2=5$
$6-1=5, 7-2=5, 8-3=5, 9-4=5, 10-5=5, ...$
$0\times5=0, 5\times0=0, 1\times5=5, 2\times5=10,$
$3\times5=15, 4\times5=20, 5\times5=25 ...$
I have **five** fingers on each hand.
Five rhymes with **hive.**
Five is an odd **number.**
There are **five letters** in the word **pizza.**

In this example, students express the number five using several different forms of text including addition, subtraction, and multiplication. For variations, they might draw representations, write a story or poem, or make long lists of things that relate to the number for their book. The idea of creating counting books using multiplication, division, or higher numbers might work best with older children.

Using riddles to describe numbers in a counting book is a good writing experience for children. Students can create their own riddle for each number, work in pairs, or the teacher could plan a class riddle book to which each child contributes a riddle for a number. Here is an example for the number three:

I am odd
I rhyme with the word free
When multiplied by eleven I equal thirty
_____.

In this representation for the number three, students could write a rhyming riddle and the teacher could prepare a riddle starter to assist reluctant writers. The idea of creating number mysteries for a counting book could be explored in Russell Hoban's *Ten What? A Mystery Counting Book.* Teachers who are interested in creating counting books with rhymes should take a look at Fritz Eichenberg's *Dancing in the Moon: Counting Rhymes.*

For those who are interested in counting books that focus on mathematical concepts, *Anno's Math Games II* by Anno is a good choice. Counting books can be used for studying money concepts.

Students could create a money book based on small amounts of change such as pennies, nickels, dimes, quarters, and half dollars. They could make rubbings of actual coins and use them to price items. For example, students could draw or cut out pictures of toys or candy bars from magazines or catalogs and match the correct amount of coins with the price tag.

The concept of time could be reinforced by having each student make a clock counting book. The teacher could prepare the face of the clock and hands for each student, or students could create their own. One page of the book could represent each hour or half hour.

Making counting books

There are endless possibilities for construction and illustration in counting books.

Books can be any size, shape, or design. Students can draw, paint, color, or cut out pictures for a collage to illustrate their number books. *The Very Best of Children's Book Illustration*, published by North Light Books, is an excellent reference for teachers to show students different types of artwork. Paul Johnson's *A Book Of One's Own: Developing Literacy Through Making Books* and *Literacy Through the Book Arts*, both published by Heinemann, are good selections that show students various ways to construct books.

Sharing and evaluation

Counting books made by students can be shared in many ways. Students from upper grades can read their books to younger students. Students from the same grade level or school district can exchange books

---

Counting book student evaluation form

Student name _____

Title of book _____
(Make a check mark next to the term that you think seems to fit the best.)

	Excellent	Good	Fair	Needs improvement
Appearance				
Theme				
Construction				

What I **liked best** about this book...

What I **liked least** about this book...

---

during SSR time. Counting books can be laminated and cataloged at the school library for continued use. Teachers can have students evaluate each other's counting books. (See student evaluation form.)

Teachers could evaluate students' counting books or students could evaluate their own work. Collecting this kind of data could be valuable in identifying students who have strengths or who are in need of improvement in certain areas. The evaluations could also be shown to parents during parent-teacher conferences.

Teachers who incorporate counting books into the curriculum will soon discover that there are no limits to their value. Teachers can use counting books to reinforce concepts, stimulate the imagination, improve literacy skills, and hopefully, strengthen all students' desire to learn.

References

Johnson, P. (1992). *A book of one's own: Developing literacy through making books.* Portsmouth, NH: Heinemann.

Johnson, P. (1993). *Literacy through the book arts.* Portsmouth, NH: Heinemann.

Society of Illustrators. (1993). *The very best of children's book illustration.* Cincinnati, OH: North Light Books.

Counting books cited

Anno, M. (1977). *Anno's math games II.* New York: Crowell.

Crews, D. (1986). *Ten black dots.* New York: Greenwillow.

Dunham, M. (1987). *Numbers: How do you say it?* New York: Lothrop, Lee & Shepard.

Eichenberg, F. (1955). *Dancing in the moon: Counting rhymes.* Orlando, FL: Harcourt Brace.

Feelings, M. (1971). *Moja means one: Swahili counting book.* New York: Dial.

Galdone, P. (1970). *The three little pigs.* New York: Seabury Press.

Galdone, P. (1972). *The three bears.* New York: Seabury Press.

Galdone, P. (1981). *The three sillies.* New York: Clarion.

Hoban, R. (1975). *Ten what? A mystery counting book.* New York: Scribner.

Krüss, J. (1972). *Three by three.* New York: Macmillan.

Laird, D. (1981). *The three little Hawaiian pigs and the magic shark.* Honolulu, HI: Barnaby.

Mack, S. (1974). *Ten bears in my bed: A goodnight countdown.* New York: Pantheon.

Rounds, G. (1993). *Three billy goats gruff.* New York: Holiday House.

Scieszka, J. (1989). *The true story of the three little pigs.* New York: Viking Kestrel.

Smith, D. (1970). *Farm numbers.* New York: Abelard.

Ungerer, T. (1962). *The three robbers.* New York: Macmillan.

Viorst, J. (1971). *The tenth good thing about Barney.* New York: Macmillan.

Other counting books

Allen, R. (1968). *Numbers: A first counting book.* New York: Platt & Monk.

Bang, M. (1983). *Ten, nine, eight.* New York: Greenwillow.

Carle, E. (1974). *My very first book of numbers.* New York: Crowell.

Chwast, S., & Moskof, M. (1971). *Still another number book.* New York: McGraw.

Crews, D. (1992). *Each orange had 8 slices.* New York: Greenwillow.

Croll, C. (1991). *The three brothers.* New York: Whitebird.

Dale, P. (1988). *Ten in the bed*. New York: Walker.

Elkin, B. (1957). *Six foolish fishermen*. Chicago: Children's Press.

Fleming, D. (1992). *Count!* New York: Henry Holt.

Garne, S.T. (1992). *One white sail*. New York: Simon & Schuster.

Hoban, T. (1972). *Count and see: 26 letters and 99 cents*. New York: Macmillan.

Keats, E. (1972). *Over in the meadow*. New York: Four Winds.

Kellogg, S. (1985). *How much is a million?* New York: Scholastic.

Kirn, A. (1966). *Nine in a line*. New York: Norton.

Kredenser, G. (1971). *One dancing drum*. Chatham, NY: Phillips.

Leydenfrost, R. (1975). *Ten little elephants*. New York: Doubleday.

Linden, A.M. (1992). *One smiling grandma*. New York: Dial.

Livermore, E. (1973). *One to ten count again*. Boston: Houghton Mifflin.

McCleod, E. (1961). *One snail and me: A book of numbers and animals and bathtubs*. Boston: Little, Brown.

McMillan, B. (1986). *Counting wildflowers*. New York: Lothrop & Lee.

Muller, R. (1992). *Hickory, dickory, dock*. New York: Scholastic.

Sendak, M. (1962). *One was Johnny: A counting book*. New York: Harper.

Seymour, B. (1969). *First counting*. New York: Walck.

Smith, D. (1970). *Farm numbers*. New York: Abelard.

Stengle, H. (1969). *Busy builders: A counting picture book*. Chicago: Children's Press.

Van Fleet, M. (1992). *One yellow lion*. New York: Dial.

Wildsmith, B. (1965). *1, 2, 3's*. New York: Watts.

Ziner, F. (1992). *Counting carnival*. New York: Putnam & Grossett.

Partner writers: A shared reading and writing experience

Lyn Bajtelsmit
Helen Naab

VOLUME 48, NUMBER 1, SEPTEMBER 1994

As elementary school teachers, we constantly seek ways to enrich our students' reading and writing experiences. Since we teach different grade levels, first grade and fifth grade, we saw the possibility of developing a shared writing program between our classes. We decided to try weekly shared writing sessions for the whole school year; our Partner Writers program was designed to help children write books.

The primary goal of our Partner Writers program was to emphasize the connection between reading and writing in a natural setting with students of different grade levels. In our project, fifth graders were paired with first graders for a weekly 30–40-minute writing session. The first grader dictated a story to the fifth grader, who transcribed it using the language of the younger child. The fifth grader also asked questions and engaged the younger writers in dialogue to clarify meaning or elicit details for the stories. Although illustrations were the first graders' responsibility, both partners often enjoyed sharing this job. Both partners included the following information on the cover of completed books (see Figure 1):

Number of the story
Title
Dictated by: (first grader's name)
Partner writer: (fifth grader's name)
Date.

Program basics

Our initial planning focused on the "how to." We decided that classes would rotate choosing partners so both classes would have the opportunity to select partners on alternate weeks. We set a regular time for weekly writing sessions. We developed special writing folders to keep track of all writing; they included record keeping, story ideas, works in progress, finished pieces of writing, and the numbers and titles of completed stories (see Figure 2). Since first graders would be paired with many fifth graders throughout the year, we decided that first graders would keep the folders, but the fifth graders assisted their first-grade partners with organizational management. The cumulative nature of the folder provided the teacher and partner with a quick overview of the writing to date. It also allowed first graders to reread their writing with new partners.

Many age-appropriate writing materials are available. We found half-lined paper to be suitable for both illustrations and text. In addition to the writing folders, several enrichment projects were incorporated into our weekly writing program to keep student interest and motivation high. For example, winter stories were written in December and illustrated, to everyone's delight, using silver glitter snow. Partners created Caldecott Book Socks (paper wind socks) to celebrate notable works of literature. First graders selected different Caldecott books and their fifth-grade partners read the books to them. Next the partners discussed their story and wrote the title, author, year it won the Caldecott award, why they liked the book, and their favorite part of the story on streamers that hung from the book sock. The book sock itself was an illustration of the story completed by the younger partner. These thematic or seasonal writing pieces were published in special Partner Writers showcase areas.

The Partner Writers connection proved so enjoyable that our relationship extended into other activities. For instance, on schoolwide Caring and Sharing Day, fifth graders wrote their own children's books to give to first-grade partners. Fifth-grade students also completed Author Study

Figure 1
Cover of student-made book

projects in which they researched themes, writing styles, and biographies of favorite children's authors and illustrators. The first graders listened to the Author Study presentations and participated in the question/answer segment.

Both teachers actively contributed to the success of each writing session. Our joint presence ensured that one of us was always available to confer, replenish materials as needed, listen to newly completed stories and congratulate the authors, and assist the partners in displaying published work. In addition, we circulated among partners and offered encouragement. Such ongoing monitoring permitted us to notice areas that needed modification or redirection. We could sense the group's need for a change of pace or an extension activity. Occasionally we matched some partners to minimize possible off-task behavior. When we detected any problems in writing, such as inappropriate topics or careless record keeping, we discussed these issues separately with the children.

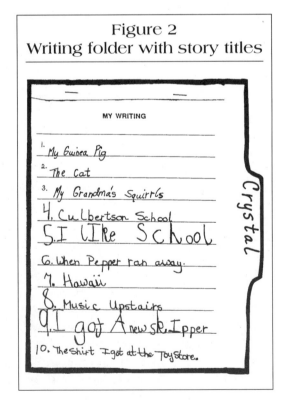

**Figure 2
Writing folder with story titles**

MY WRITING

1. My Guinea Pig
2. The Cat
3. My Grandma's Squirrls
4. Culbertson School
5. I LIke School
6. When Pepper ran away.
7. Hawaii
8. Music Upstairs
9. I got A new sk.Ipper
10. The shirt I got at the Toy Store.

Crystal

Signs of success

The one-to-one pairing of student writers is a powerful connection. Before our first writing session, we prepared our classes individually for what to expect. The first few meetings led to a level of comfort and trust that grew throughout the year. Many parents reported that their children often talked about Partner Writers at home. One child was even reluctant to miss school on Partner Writers' day!

Partner rotation gave all students the experience of working with a variety of people. However, some unique partnerships evolved, and we encouraged them to continue working together as they moved toward collaboration in their writing. With writing being modeled in such a personal way, first graders soon began transferring some of the mechanics demonstrated into their own written work. This move toward independent writing empowered the first graders, while the fifth graders gained a greater understanding of story framework, sense of audience, and purpose for writing. As one fifth grader stated, "I have enjoyed Partner Writers because you can get to know younger kids and what kind of writing they like."

Minilessons helped fifth graders develop questioning techniques and interpersonal skills. For instance, a minilesson on questioning techniques encouraged fifth graders to think ahead and to generate questions that might be asked to get more information from the first graders about their stories. In this way, the teacher helped them prepare for the writing session and modeled for them the supportive and encouraging role they could play. This focus on questioning strategies prompted one fifth grader to reflect on his own writing and notice that "Partner Writers has taught me to ask questions before I write."

To us, our Partner Writers program was a wonderful, successful venture. In spite of the general movement and activity in the classroom, the writers remained focused. The attention of each pair was intensely directed to the writing process in a lively, dynamic way.

The second year

As a result of Partner Writers, our bond of collegiality was strengthened, and we developed many exciting new ideas for the next school year. However, when one of us was reassigned to another elementary school within the district, we modified our plans. For instance, the first- and fifth-grade partners now get together only once a month for a joint writing session. During the interim weeks, we rely on the district's school-to-school mail system to keep the writing connection alive.

In September, prior to our first face-to-face writing session, students sent letters of introduction to one another. Fifth graders composed personal letters, and first graders drew illustrations of themselves and wrote a sentence or two describing their pictures. Next, fifth graders designed a survey that both classes completed. Fifth graders then made colorful charts and graphs to interpret the results and shared them at our first meeting. The children enjoyed learning that baseball was the favorite sport, April had the greatest number of student birthdays, and pizza was by far the favorite food!

Another special activity was compiling an anthology of short stories written by the partners. Two copies of the anthology were written and illustrated so each class could have its own. The focus on Caldecott books was maintained, but the writing project was redesigned as a cross-grade response to shared literature. Within our own classrooms, we gathered together the same selection of Caldecott books. Prior to our meeting, students read and responded in writing to a Caldecott book of their choice. When they met for Partner Writers, students had fun discovering who their partner was by looking for the other student who had read the same book. Partners then reread the story, shared their individual responses, wrote a joint summary, and designed and illustrated a cover.

Looking back over our experiences with Partner Writers during the past 2 years, we see that shared writing can take many forms. Initially, our program was developed for students within the same school. Happily we learned that a shared writing program can be easily implemented with students of different grade levels even when they attend different schools. The direction the program takes will be shaped by the needs and interests of the students. With forethought, reflection, and vision, the opportunities are endless!

Navigating the writing process: Strategies for young children

Candace C. Poindexter
Irene R. Oliver

VOLUME 52, NUMBER 4, DECEMBER 1998/JANUARY 1999

Picture yourself in your third-grade classroom. You've labored over a creative writing assignment for several days, and you're anxiously awaiting your teacher's feedback. When she returns your paper, all you are aware of is a bunch of red marks all over it. You thought your paper was pretty good, but obviously your teacher had a different opinion. You feel devastated. All of your hard work is awash in a tidal wave of red ink.

Does that sound familiar? Fortunately, children today may be having a different experience when it comes to writing. While elementary school teachers have always been concerned with children's literacy, in the past most of our efforts were devoted to helping children read rather than to write (Chomsky, 1971; Sealey, Sealey, & Millmore, 1979). "Between the mid-1960's and the late 1970's, 'creative writing' appeared as a curricular issue [in elementary schools] because many students clearly were not being exposed to composition before high school" (Stice, Bertrand, & Bertrand, 1995, p. 213). Most school-age children look forward to the new experience of learning to write, and, if handled sensitively, the earliest stages of writing are welcomed (Sealey et al., 1979).

Donald Graves (1983) reached two important conclusions in the late 1970s. He recognized that children seemed to write more on unassigned topics as compared to teacher-assigned topics, and that they appeared to go through three general stages in writing: prewriting, writing, and postwriting. As a result of Graves's research, the writing process, as we know it, was identified. The previously well-known practice of having children turn in a single draft on an assigned topic to be graded and corrected by the teacher was no longer considered good teaching (Stice et al., 1995).

The writing process, when implemented in the classroom, has been referred to as the authoring cycle (Calkins, 1986; Harp & Brewer, 1996; Newman, 1984; Stice et al., 1995). Instead of being looked at as a linear process, Harp and

Brewer (1996) have described the process as being recursive.

> The writer decides, for example, what to write, begins the piece, changes plans for the writing, and decides on another purpose. Then she begins writing again. Long before the piece is finished, words are deleted and thoughts are reexpressed in different language. Sometimes, as the piece unfolds, the purpose, design, or even the audience may change. Therefore, pieces of writing may be abandoned along the way and never reach their intended audience. (p. 83)

This recursive process engages both the teacher and the student in authentic kinds of writing, is purposely written for a known audience, and is performed every day. The writing process has typically been thought to be the domain of the upper grades. However, it no longer is necessary to wait until children can read before they begin to write (Sealey et al., 1979). Using simple frameworks, introductions to the process, and activities involved in each stage, even primary students can effectively use the writing process. For younger students, each stage of the process needs to be modeled, ending up with a brief paragraph or composition. Additionally, students need to learn the procedures, frameworks, terminologies, and activities involved in each step of the writing process. They need to learn how to use the prewriting frameworks and the peer revision and editing forms and then be provided with opportunities to practice each procedure (Tomkins, 1990).

The writing process

Prewriting. Prewriting is the getting-ready-to-write stage (Tompkins, 1990). This is the time for the writer to decide on the topic and to gather and organize his/her ideas. In the authoring cycle, prewriting begins with the children's lives, their reading, and events in the daily life of the classroom (Stice et al., 1995). Prewriting is often neglected but is crucial. According to Donald Murray (1982), 70% or more of writing time should be spent in prewriting.

Prewriting for kindergarten and early first-grade students is often a picture that they draw before they write. For more mature primary students, however, prewriting can be introduced using a variety of frameworks. Two such frameworks are the Star Organizer and the Step Map.

The *star organizer* (Figure 1) helps students organize their thoughts when writing a description. The framework is then used as a map for the paragraph they write. Modeling is always important, but especially so when helping young children understand the writing process. Figure 1 shows an example of a teacher's star organizer used to describe her dog, Sadie. The teacher wrote down phrases next to each point of the star that corresponded to the points she wanted to make in her paragraph about her dog.

The teacher then modeled for the students how to write a paragraph from the star organizer, explaining about transition words, and rearranging and joining sentences. Following is a paragraph written using the above organizer:

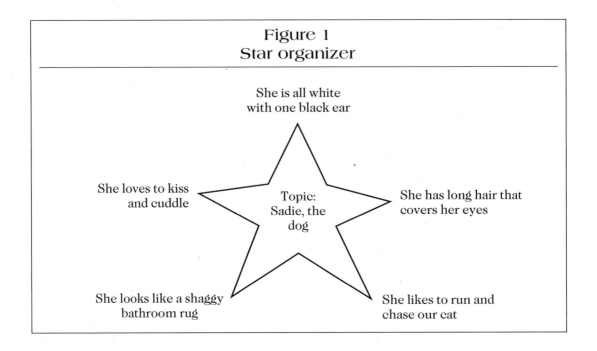

**Figure 1
Star organizer**

She is all white
with one black ear

She loves to kiss
and cuddle

Topic:
Sadie, the
dog

She has long hair that
covers her eyes

She looks like a shaggy
bathroom rug

She likes to run and
chase our cat

My dog Sadie is all white with one black ear. Her hair is so long that it covers her eyes and makes her look like a shaggy bathroom rug. Sadie is very playful and likes to chase our cat, but she also loves to cuddle and kiss.

Children are then given their own blank star organizer and asked to describe something or someone. As a test of their descriptive abilities, students can attempt to draw a picture from their partner's paragraph. It's fun to see another's perception of one's description.

Another writing framework applicable for primary grades is the *step map*. This is ideal for writing directions or sequencing. To introduce this organizer, children are asked to observe while the teacher makes a peanut butter and jelly sandwich. They are then asked to describe what they just saw as the teacher fills in the step map (see Figure 2).

The same procedure described above is followed as the teacher models how to use the step map as a guide to write a paragraph about making a peanut butter and jelly sandwich.

Drafting. In the drafting stage, the students actually write and refine their paragraphs or compositions. "It is imperative that during the composing and drafting phase the focus is on the creation and communication of meaning, not on the mechanics" (Harp & Brewer, 1996, p. 88). These beginning drafts provide students and teachers with something to work with, and therefore spelling, punctuation, capitalization, and sentence structure should not be stressed. Children should be "encouraged to get their words and ideas on paper and attempt to spell whatever words they want to use" (Stice et al., 1995, p. 216). Limiting words to ones students can spell dramatically reduces the quality of young children's writings. Students should also be instructed to write on every other line of their papers to allow room for revising and editing.

Revising/editing. Revising deals with the content of the written piece, while editing produces a readable text and deals with proofreading tasks. At the revision stage, writers refine and polish what they have written. This can include text reorganization (cutting and pasting), word choice, changes in sentence structure, or other additions and deletions. Editing deals with the mechanics of writing such

as spelling and punctuation. Young children who are just figuring out what a sentence is can be responsible for checking one or two elements of their writing. Older and more experienced writers often use peers to help them revise and edit. In the early primary grades, however, the revision and editing stages are often collapsed together. Since young children are usually not critical readers, they need simple suggestions to help get them through these two stages. The forms reproduced below help students focus on specific areas of writing and categories of errors. Figure 3 is an example of a job sheet that is ideal for first- and second-grade students who have just been introduced to the writing process.

Figures 4 and 5 are appropriate for more mature writers who have been exposed to some of the more sophisticated

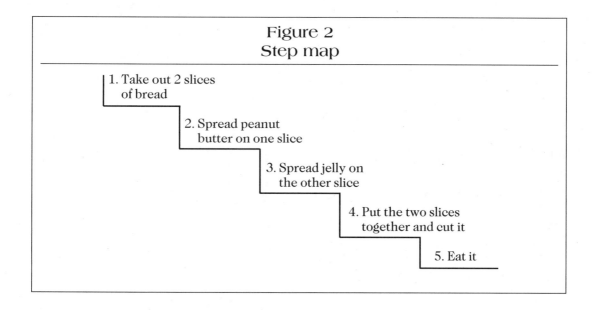

Figure 2
Step map

1. Take out 2 slices of bread
2. Spread peanut butter on one slice
3. Spread jelly on the other slice
4. Put the two slices together and cut it
5. Eat it

aspects of language. The Partner's Revision Form (Figure 4) is a good tool to begin the introduction of peer revision, while the Proofreading Checklist (Figure 5) encourages children to perform basic editing tasks.

After peer revision and editing have taken place, students should confer with the teacher before they move to the final step. For young children, merely reading their draft to their teacher is considered to be a form of conferring. The student and the teacher can talk about the piece, make suggestions for improvements, and discuss options for publication.

Publishing. The purpose of publishing is to share and celebrate finished products (Stice et al., 1995). Students publish their writings by sharing them with an audience in the final stage of the writing process. Whether publishing is by creating a bound class book or by reading the piece to an audience, this is a stage that should not be skipped. Inviting parents and/or grandparents to listen to children read their finished products is another wonderful example of publishing. By sharing their writing, students develop sensitivity to an audience and confidence in themselves as authors (Tomkins, 1990). Some suggestions for primary publishing include:

- classroom newspapers,
- puppet shows and plays,
- cookbooks,
- author's chair,
- advertisements and signs,
- a variety of books (e.g., accordion, pop-up, shape, etc.), and
- displays (e.g., book jackets, clothes hanger mobiles, windsocks, door-knob hangers, and sun visors).

Published works should be available in the classroom or in the school library for children to read and reread.

Figure 3
Job sheet

My writing job sheet

Your name _____

Today's date _____

1. Read your draft to yourself.
2. Read your draft to a friend.
3. Put on your editing hat.
   Edit your draft for:
   _____ spelling
   _____ capital letters
4. Put your draft in our *Publishing Box*.

Figure 4
Partner's revision form

I read _____'s paper.

His/her topic is _____.

This paper has the following elements:

     An interesting, "catchy" beginning _____

     Good supporting details   _____

     A logical conclusion   _____

The best thing about my partner's paper is _____

_____

If my partner wanted to change something, I would suggest _____

_____

Figure 5
Proofreading checklist

( ) 1. Did I spell all words correctly?

( ) 2. Did I write each sentence as a complete thought?

( ) 3. Did I begin each sentence with a capital letter?

( ) 4. Did I use capital letters correctly in other places?

( ) 5. Did I indent each paragraph?

Younger children are motivated by stories and love to see their own stories "published." However, laborious recopying is not suggested for very young children as their final drafts are likely to have as many or more errors as the draft they are correcting. "One rule of thumb says for the very youngest writers, do not attempt corrections; for experienced kindergartners, one correction per project is enough, and so on" (Harp & Brewer, 1996, p. 96). Many teachers and students like to use a word processor for their draft to make revising and editing easier.

The writing process is complex but not so complex as to be beyond the reach of young children. "Children tend to learn to write faster, better, and more joyfully when they do so for their own purposes, under the guidance and encouragement of a knowledgeable teacher" (Stice et al., 1995, p. 251). Using the strategies described above, your students will eagerly look forward to writing and publishing.

REFERENCES

Calkins, L. (1986). *The art of teaching writing.* Portsmouth, NH: Heinemann.

Chomsky, C. (1971). Write first, read later. *Childhood Education, 47,* 296–299.

Graves, D. (1983). *Writing: Teachers and children at work.* Portsmouth, NH: Heinemann.

Harp, B., & Brewer, J. (1996). *Reading and writing: Teaching for the connections.* Fort Worth, TX: Harcourt Brace.

Murray, D.H. (1982). *Learning by teaching.* Montclair, NJ: Boynton/Cook.

Newman, J. (1984). *The craft of children's writing.* Portsmouth, NH: Heinemann.

Sealey, L., Sealey, N., & Millmore, M. (1979). *Children's writings.* Newark, DE: International Reading Association.

Stice, C., Bertrand, J., & Bertrand, N. (1995). *Integrating reading and the other language arts.* Belmont, CA: Wadsworth.

Tompkins, G. (1990). *Teaching writing: Balancing process and product.* New York: Macmillan.

An author's storyboard technique as a prewriting strategy

Suzanne L. Harrington

VOLUME 48, NUMBER 3, NOVEMBER 1994

After several years of teaching children to write through a process approach, we saw that the overall quality of writing in our school had much improved, but fictional writing was still an area of frustration. Children seemed motivated to attempt this genre, but they frequently had difficulty making their stories believable. Teachers also found that many students got carried away, writing page after page with no direction or destination. Without an ending or adequate storyline at their disposal, they often ended their stories by promising a new chapter or sequel to explain everything.

By definition, the writing process is based on the strategies writers use to compose. Peter Catalanotto, an author who has had success both in writing and illustrating children's stories, came to our school to talk about how a published author creates her/his stories. His presentation centered on his storyboard technique, the process he uses to write stories.

The storyboard is a prewriting technique that combines children's love of drawing with their storytelling prowess.

Peter displayed his storyboard for his first published book, *Dylan's Day Out* (1989), which consisted of a large sheet of paper divided into sections upon which he had sketched out scenes from the story.

Using Peter's presentation as a model, I conducted follow-up lessons involving the storyboard technique to help students write fictional stories. To help them get started, I constructed a blank storyboard frame by dividing a piece of plain white paper into several sections. I reminded the children about the tips Peter Catalanotto had shared with them as writers:

- Draw your story ideas on a storyboard while thinking through a story.

- Sketch your story; save your fine detailed drawings for the published version. (A writer may not want to revise works of art.)

- Often characters in good stories have a goal and, after encountering problems reaching that goal, find a solution to end the story. Think through the goal and solution first, because they will guide the guts of the story.

- Write about known topics, and you will write with authority.
- Create stories with unusual twists so that people will want to read them.
- Ground fantasy stories in reality to make them believable.

The children used workshop time to brainstorm ideas about their topics and roughly sketch out stories on the storyboard frames, remembering to think through their beginnings and endings first. Some children found they needed more than the number of sections I had provided, a problem the children solved by adapting the storyboard frames to their needs. When the children were satisfied with the storylines they created, they were ready to put words to paper.

The children were reminded of Peter's writing tips during minilessons before each workshop session. For instance, we looked at favorite picture books to see if Peter's tips held true for other authors as well. Children noticed the unusual twists and reacted to the ways authors made their stories work. The children began to make an important connection between writing and reading by discussing how books may have begun as writers' storyboards.

A storyboard or the resulting written draft can be revised at any stage. Children often revised their storylines before the drafting even began because they were encouraged to share their storyboards with others, to talk out the stories, thereby thinking through missing pieces and questionable details. .

Reluctant writers found the storyboard strategy motivational. Todd, a fifth grader, preferred fiction over personal narrative, but prior to his use of storyboards, his stories were farfetched, with unresolved storylines. Using a storyboard, he sketched out a story about a familiar topic, his two pet cats. He began by sketching his main characters' goal—Ramona and Calvin, his two barn cats, wanted to sneak into the farmhouse for warmth and adventure. Todd then sketched the ending of the story—the cats' narrow escape through a crack in the basement window back to the barn before being discovered by their owner. Working quickly during the storyboard creation, he found that the events of the story began to fall into place, because he had given thought to the ending.

Todd created a fantasy in which cats and mice talked and reasoned, but his animals were believable because he gave them real animal attributes. For instance, Todd's cats really do try to get into the house on cold winter days. Todd said during sharing time that he had never read a story like the one he created, and he thought others would enjoy reading it.

Many of our remedial students have great difficulty writing. The storyboard technique provided an impetus to write by using art as a way to express their ideas. Jed, a fourth grader, often sat through whole class periods appearing overwhelmed, claiming to be stuck for an idea or thinking. His teacher told me that by December he had accomplished very little and had not published anything.

Figure 1
Todd's story board

Figure 2
Todd's story, typed with spelling and punctuation errors

First draft

Calvin the Clawless and Ramona the Brave

Hi my name is Ramona the Brave. I was named Ramona the Brave because I have to stand up to Rusty the dog. I'll be telling the story.

"And I'm Calvin the..."

"Clue less," shouts Ramona.

"Be queit Ramona, I'm Calvin the Clawless and I am called that because I don't have front claws."

Ramona started to talk. "Our story begins one day in the winter. I was conserving my energy by sleeping when Calvin jumped on me and kept saying, "The door is open! the door is open!"

So I followed him inside the house where we left out dirty, wet, footprints on the new rug. We found the door to the basement open so we whent down the steps into The Basement.

I was hungrey and when I saw a mouse right in front of me I natruly and gracefully sprang through the air and .... stopped in midflight when Calvin jumped in front of me and Hissed at me.

"I did not Ramona, I just told you not to hurt them because they where my friends," said Calvin.

"Be q-u-i-e-t Calvin," Ramona Hissed then continued.

While I was still hungrey and thinking of the dogs full dish of food, we met the mice.

Chapter 2 The Mice

The mice told us to come into their hole which was just big enough for Calvin and I.

One young mouse named Fred had races with me to see who could climb the fastest and Calvin played an older mouse in one on one soccer with a sawdust ball and a super strong spider web net.

I was still hungrey so I asked the mice where the dogs dish was.

"They showed it—we ate it," exclaimed Calvin.

"Be quiet Calvin," Ramona yelled. Calvin crossed his paws.

Well anyway... Then we whent to our master Todd's room and watched t.v. and played N.E.S.

"She thought the things on the screen were meant for her to catch so she tried to catch them but she slammed her face in to the screen," laughed Calvin.

Who's telling the story me or you Calvin, well um now were was I ... oh yea ... well soon our master's mom came home and if she would have found us, I wouldn't be telling this story right now. The mice showed us a way out though a crack in the wall and we were home free.

The end.

However, the storyboard technique allowed him to use his penchant for drawing and his love of animals to his advantage. He was more motivated to write this story than any other piece previously started. The day he shared his illustrated picture book entitled *Desert Rats* with his class he received many accolades. This taste of success may have been the catalyst he needed to grow as a writer.

The first time students used the storyboard strategy, many of their topics were fantasies about animals having adventures and then returning to their homes, borrowing from Peter Catalanotto's *Dylan's Day Out* (1989). However, most children soon began to see how storyboards could be used to create fictional stories on many topics. Fifth-grader Kurt sketched a piece about a personal goal to own a rare baseball card and how he fictitiously went about acquiring it. Misty, a third grader, invented a family of bears who found themselves trapped under a collapsing bridge. She modeled the bears' personalities upon those of her three sisters, and she told her classmates that she was thinking about writing a series of bear family stories. Fernanda created a storyline about a penguin who couldn't swim; she used what she had learned from reading *Mr. Popper's Penguins* (Atwater & Atwater, 1938) to develop her fictional piece.

Most of the children who tried the storyboard technique were pleased with the results. Todd was able to express why he was successful with the storyboard. "Finding the end and the beginning are the hardest parts. Once I get into the story, it's easy to write, but when I get to where it should end, I just can't stop the story. If I know the ending before I write, it's easier to stop."

Jed said, "It was fun. It made me think while I was drawing." These writers are learning that thinking about a story is an important part of the writing process. Lucy Calkins (1986) calls this process "rehearsal," a term she attributes to Donald Graves (1983). She states, "Sometimes during rehearsal, writers map possible lines of development for their pieces, or sketch out the patterns in their ideas. Often they rehearse by talking, observing, or reading. During all of this, they experience a growing readiness to put themselves on the line" (p. 17). We saw evidence that our students were empowered to succeed by sketching their stories. Their feelings of success proved to them that the time it takes is worth it.

The true test that a strategy is successful, however, is in seeing children use the technique when needed without direction. During subsequent workshops, I saw children nod their heads when they heard teachers say that Peter's storyboard ideas could be used for a lifetime of writing. Many of the students asked to keep a storyboard frame in their writing folders so they could sketch out future ideas. On their own, others divided blank paper into sections before sketching. Our students had indeed added the storyboard technique to their repertoire of prewriting strategies.

REFERENCES

Atwater, R., & Atwater, F. (1938). *Mr. Popper's penguins*. New York: Dell.

Calkins, L. (1986). *The art of teaching writing*. Portsmouth, NH: Heinemann.

Graves, D. (1983). *Writing: Teachers & children at work*. Portsmouth, NH: Heinemann.

Catalanotto, P. (1989). *Dylan's day out*. New York: Orchard Books.

Catalanotto, P. (1990). *Mr. Mumble*. New York: Orchard Books.

BOOKS WRITTEN AND ILLUSTRATED BY PETER CATALANOTTO

Catalanotto, P. (1991). *Christmas always*. New York: Orchard Books.

What's in a name?

Sandy K. Biles

VOLUME 50, NUMBER 7, APRIL 1997

The book *The House on Mango Street* by Sandra Cisneros is written in short vignettes of a young girl growing up in the Latino section of Chicago. Several of these short essays make excellent writing prompts for older students.

A good writing selection for early September is the chapter "My Name." In this vignette, Esperanza shares what her name means in English and in Spanish, explains how the name was chosen for her by her parents, and tells how much trouble everyone at school has pronouncing *Esperanza*. She discusses her desire to change her name: "I would like to baptize myself under a new name, a name more like the real me, the one nobody sees." Many students can identify with her wish for a different name.

After reading this piece, students ask their parents about their own names—where they came from, how they were chosen, what they mean—and then write about their discoveries. The students tell what names they would choose, if they could choose new names, and why.

This exercise provides a good beginning writing experience for the year, which goes into the portfolio, and gives insight into who my students are and how they see themselves.

REFERENCE

Cisneros, S. (1991). *The house on Mango Street.* New York: Vintage.

Fairy tales—a vehicle of literacy

Maggie Hoagland

VOLUME 47, NUMBER 4, DECEMBER 1993/JANUARY 1994

After reading the mail included within the pages of *The Jolly Postman* by Janet and Allan Ahlberg, my Grade 6 students were eager to write their own notes to storybook characters from other book characters.

Students chose favorite characters, whether very evil or very good, and began writing notes, postcards, coupons and invitations. Envelopes were appropriately and creatively addressed. (This provided the class with a perfect opportunity to review letter-writing strategies.) Amy wrote to Rapunzel:

Dear Rapunzel,

You may have heard of me. My name is Stiffle Stratanugu. I'm a famous hair stylist.

I live on a creek past the woods. I've done Goldilocks's hair. Actually, I turned her blond and nicknamed her Goldilocks. Have you heard of Cinderella? That night she went to the ball, her fairy godmother didn't do everything. I helped with the hair!

Anyway, when I did Sleeping Beauty's hair (she's a real gossiper), she said you had beautiful blonde hair. Well, what I'm trying to say is that I don't think of you as a blonde. When I hear the name Rapunzel, oh, Rapunzel, I think...blue or green hair. So, think it over. Have your people call my people and we'll make an appointment. We could wash, dry, and dye!!! Give my regards to the prince!

Love ya,
Stiffle Stratanugu

S. Stratanugu
1 Creek Waterway
Past the Woods

Rapunzel Stapunzel
1801 Blondie Drive
The Big Palace

City Hall
c/o Dept. of Urban Development
1 Hill Road
Grassville 01234

D.Troll
1 Under the Bridge
Grassville 01234

Josh wrote a letter to the Troll who bothered the Billy Goats Gruff:

City Hall
c/o Dept. of Urban Development
1 Hill Road
Grassville 01234

Dear Dee Troll,

We have written to tell you that your home under the bridge is CONDEMNED! We will be putting in a suspension bridge, high-rise apartments, and hotels. We also have the best lawyer in Grassville working on the Billy Goat Gruff Case. Once again, you must move out of your house.

Sorry for the inconvenience.

Yours truly,
John Condemner
Director of Urban Development

After the letters were shared, a team of students sorted them and wrote a narrative in poetic form about the postman delivering each letter. This story was then printed, illustrated, and bound into a big book.

The class now proudly shares its big book of storybook letters with other classes and will be donating it to the town library at the end of the year.

Phantasy Phacts: Creative writing from another perspective

Roman Taraban
Cynthia Orengil

VOLUME 50, NUMBER 2, OCTOBER 1996

Teachers and students often develop a sense of connection, worth, and deep affection. When students demonstrate insight, creativity, and enthusiasm as they develop academic skills, students and teachers feel a sense of accomplishment. Over the past 2 years, we have been exploring ways to strengthen student/teacher bonds through creative writing.

Creative writing requires a goal. Children like to entertain through their writing or to express clear and simple emotions. Phantasy Phacts was a schoolwide creative writing activity that developed into a highly successful way for students to write about something potentially important, interesting, or funny. The first time we tried this idea, the topic was teachers.

The objective of the activity was to get all of the pupils from Grades 1–9 to write about their teacher's early life. Drawings were encouraged. The assignment was ungraded so that the students would feel free to let their imaginations soar. In order to

achieve schoolwide participation, the principal circulated the activity sheet to all of the teachers as a writing and drawing project. We provided a set of guidelines and encouraged students and teachers to add their own suggestions.

Students' work was collected and displayed. Students stopped with their friends to read the "Phacts" about teachers and to comment on the texts and pictures. The Home and School Association selected winning stories, and ribbons were displayed with the submissions. The students' work was developed into a presentation for a faculty appreciation dinner by creating a script that consisted largely of selections from the children's stories (see the example by Sarah). Color slides were made of students' drawings and were projected onto a screen while the students' work was read aloud.

There was much laughter as teachers and parents listened to the students' imaginative and incisive stories. Even though the teachers were now punctual, well mannered, and respected, it turned out that the students portrayed some as dawdlers when their mothers called and as rowdy and mischievous at school. One student speculated that her teacher's hardest decision each morning was "What color should I wear today?" Another student suggested that when her teacher was young, she loved to sew; she even sewed her own pajamas. She was also a perfectionist. "Her room was always neat and tidy. If anything was out of place it was because her brother had been in her room."

We heard of the teacher with the pet chicken named Cluck Cluck. "Cluck Cluck walked with her to school every day...[Mrs. P.] always felt better when Cluck Cluck was with her." And there was Mrs. N. who

---

Phantasy Phacts assignment sheet

A. Draw a picture of your teacher when he or she was your age. Use a standard size sheet of paper and the drawing materials of your choice (e.g., markers, crayons, pencils, watercolors).
B. If you are a younger student, then simply answer the questions below. If you are an older student, use the questions as a guide and write a 1–3 paragraph description of one of your teachers. You can use your imagination in more than one way for this activity. For example, you might want to make the description humorous. Another possibility is to try to imagine what your teacher's life was really like. You could also do research from books, movies, and magazines to find out what daily life may have been like for your teacher.
C. Submit the picture and written description to your teacher.

A Day in the Life of My Teacher When She (He) Was My Age
1. How old is your teacher in this description?
2. Where does your teacher live (apartment, house, farm)?
3. What does your teacher's bedroom look like?
4. What did your teacher dress up in this morning?
5. What did your teacher have for breakfast?
6. Did your teacher brush her teeth, comb his hair, etc.?
7. How did your teacher get to school?
8. What is your teacher's favorite subject?
9. What is your teacher's favorite story book?
10. Is your teacher a good student?
11. What does your teacher usually daydream about in school?
12. What does your teacher like to have for lunch?
13. Does your teacher have pets?
14. Does your teacher get along with brothers and sisters?
15. What is your teacher's favorite color, TV show, pizza topping, etc.?
16. What chores does your teacher do?
17. What does your teacher's mother say to him/her?
18. What does your teacher's father say to him/her?
19. Who are your teacher's friends?
20. Does your teacher spend any money?

Sample student writing about her teacher

When Mrs. Lara was my age, 12, she lived in a little town called Mineral Wells. Everyday she would wake up and get ready for school. She'd pick one pair of shorts out of the many colored she had with the little white strips going down the sides. To finish the outfit she'd add the little colored shirt with the white stripes down the shoulder to match. Her hardest decision of the morning was "What color should I wear today?" She would wear her hair in "trensas" with little red bows.

When she was in school she would daydream about becoming a Tejano singer. At lunch she would give performances of her favorite tejano songs. When she was listening to the radio she would be listening to Laura Canales and Little Joe. Every day she would practice with her brothers and sisters, the "cumbia."

All in all Mrs. Lara grew up like kids these days, having the same dreams and expectations, even though times were different back then. She did not follow her dream of becoming a Tejano singer, instead she became a teacher.

Sarah Silvas

was a perfect student. She was not in any athletics. When she had free time on her hand she would read books or dance. Mrs. [N.] also gave good advice. When somebody was mean to her she would forgive them. She was the type of person who would go around saying, "If God was here would you be doing this."

We believe that this activity was a success because it allowed students to write about something that was important to them in a nonthreatening way. Teachers enjoyed seeing themselves through their students' eyes. The Phantasy Phacts idea has also led to some fascinating suggestions for related writing projects in our schools.

The Phantasy Phacts assignment sheet that we used in our project could be easily adapted for historical characters. For instance, students could write about a day in the life of a youthful Christopher Columbus, or they could write about a day in the life of a young Pilgrim or Native American. It could also be used to get children to speculate about current public figures.

Author note

We would like to thank Roberta Meyer, Maureen Lambert, and members of the Home and School association at Christ the King Cathedral School for their help with this activity.

Form poems for tired words

Terry Henkelman

Volume 50, Number 5, February 1997

Spice up tired adjectives and verbs with form poems. Consult a thesaurus to develop poems for overused words. Below you will see a sample word poem for the adjective *funny*.

Develop a list of other overused adjectives with your class. Have students select a word from the list and write their own word poem. Discuss with your class how these poems can improve their writing when they replace common words with new and exciting words.

Other word form poems can include verbs or antonyms. For verbs use the word *to* in front of each synonym. Here are some examples of these poems:

FUNNY...
So amusing
So comical
So humorous
So mirthful
So laughable
Sooo...funny

WISH...
To want
To desire
To crave
To long
To hope
To yearn
Tooo...wish

FUNNY is...
Not serious
Not grave
Not sober
Not dignified

Try form poems with your class and help students say good-bye to tired words.

Surprise me:
The poetry of wet paint

David M. Salyer

VOLUME 50, NUMBER 7, APRIL 1997

Long sheets of clean plastic lined the edges of the hallway outside of our classroom. As part of a larger inquiry on motion, first and second graders spent several weeks designing and building gravity-powered vehicles out of cereal boxes, jar lids, rubber bands, and other materials. Now the axles were in place, the wheels were finally turning, and the bodies were taped and glued. Painting the last bright strokes of color, the children carefully placed their wet vehicles on the plastic to dry. As more children completed their painting and parked their vehicles next to the others, they voiced concerns about the other classrooms. Recess was coming. Soon other children would be rushing past our room to the playground. Would they leave our vehicles alone? Could we be sure that our vehicles would not be stepped on or touched?

"We could vote for someone to go and tell them to be careful."

"Yeah, but what if they forget?"

"Hey, someone could just stand in the hall and tell them!"

"But then they would miss recess."

"Besides, we couldn't stay in the hall all the time and tell everybody!"

Still wondering what to do, the group of worried children moved back into the room to clean up, except for Zach and Kyle.

"Can we make a sign?"

Since other children were still working, I agreed, thinking a new project would keep the early finishers occupied. But very quickly the boys' sign making began to echo around the room. Watching others abandon cleanup to join in, I suddenly realized that I had given little thought to this kind of text making. Students' energy was high as signs were written, colored, and posted in our hallway. I looked over their shoulders with interest as individuals and small groups created signs that read:

Do not touch
Be wary or you'll be sorry

Caution
Toxic Paint

Warning
Wet Paint

Wet Paint

Do not touch
Warning wet paint

Be careful
Wet Paint

Please
Do not touch!!!

Do not touch

Why had I not thought about this kind of writing before? Watching these engaged children, I wondered what it was they were doing and what it all meant.

Understanding children's sign making

Children's spontaneous sign making has been mentioned and examined in the literature (Bissex, 1980; Newkirk, 1989; Taylor, 1983). What is especially noteworthy is the children's preoccupation with either the process of making signs or with sign writing as an "intermediary form" (Newkirk, 1989, p. 7) that children work in as they acquire competence in forms or modes that are different than stories. How do we classify the kind of writing that children engage in when they compose a sign? It certainly is not narrative, the kind of writing found typically in the classroom. Newkirk (1989) concludes that in sign writing, children engage in either persuasive or regulatory discourse.

Signs that are composed to control or influence the behavior of others are written in the regulatory mode. This is writing that holds power and can change the behavior of those who read the sign in certain contexts (e.g., *Do not touch*). Those signs that couple a demand with a reason shift to the persuasive mode (e.g., *Be careful Wet Paint*).

In the persuasive mode, the writer cannot take for granted that the behavior of the reader will change. The signs require more message to influence others. Further, the signs that children compose in either the regulatory or persuasive modes are not simply autonomous texts (texts that are free standing and unrelated to anything else) but are determined by the situational context in which they occur and by the larger cultural context that shapes both the situation and the form of writing (Kinneavy, 1971; Vygotsky, 1978). They have reference to a situation, the reality in which they are embedded.

Looking back at the signs the children composed, I found that they could be classified as either persuasive or regulatory:

Persuasive mode

Do not touch
Be wary or you'll be sorry

Warning
Wet Paint

Do not touch
Warning wet paint

Be careful
Wet Paint

Please
Do not touch!!!

Regulatory mode

Do not touch

Wet Paint

Most of the signs were written in the persuasive mode, which includes additional language intended to convince the reader to leave the freshly painted vehicles alone. Looking again at the signs the children made, I was disturbed by one of the persuasive pieces. It seemed that it was more than a sign intended simply to persuade a reader to engage in a particular course of action. This sign was clearly more distant from the immediate reality of wet paint. This sign referred to a fictional world.

Caution
Toxic Paint

Though the message seems small, it says big things about the writing of children and what they control. What this sign refers to clearly does not exist. The common water-based school paint is not toxic, and the two children who wrote it (and also many of the children and adults who read it) knew that.

In this literacy event, the "edges" of the discourse became "unpredictable" (Barthes, 1975, p. 36) and shifted or turned a corner. Here language, rather than calling attention to something else, was in fact calling attention to itself. And we call that kind of text *literature* (Kinneavy, 1971). The sign *Caution Toxic Paint* has done away with its own genre (Barthes, 1975); the text moved while it was saying something about the world and became poetry.

Sign making modes of engagement and surprise

In schools and in daily life people frequently engage in written texts in five distinguishable ways or modes: performative, functional, informational, recreational, and the epistemic (Wells & Chang-Wells, 1992). The children's sign writing and reading moved among at least three of these modes of engagement: the performative (encoding the sign), the functional (the sign as a means to an end), and the informational (the sign as a source of information). With the shift from the prose of wet paint to the poetry of toxic paint, we can include two more ways some of the children were engaged with their texts: the recreational (the sign as an enjoyable end in itself) and the epistemic (the sign as transactional). An epistemic engagement with *Caution Toxic Paint* invites the writer/ reader into a dialogue "with the text to interpret its meaning" (Wells & Chang-Wells, 1992, p. 140). Those children and their readers who were involved with the signs in recreational epistemic ways were more fully exploring the power of written language.

Successful communication usually requires that we post a tacit *No Surprises Allowed*. Readers and writers need the predictable meanings implied in a situation to help make meaning (Halliday & Hasan, 1989). But *Caution Toxic Paint* invites surprise. The sign is more than a warning, and we read it differently. It takes us elsewhere, inviting us into the pleasures of poetry. And I nearly missed it!

As teachers, we need to assume a particular stance in our classrooms, and that stance must read *Surprise Me!* For it's only our "act[s] of recognition" (Fish, 1980, p. 326) that will allow us to interpret the rich surprises offered by children.

"Can we make a sign?"

Yes!

REFERENCES

Barthes, R. (1975). *The pleasures of the text.* (R. Miller, Trans.). New York: Farrar, Straus & Giroux.

Bissex, G. (1980). *Gnys at wrk: A child learns to write and read.* Cambridge, MA: Harvard University Press.

Fish, S. (1980). *Is there a text in this class?* Cambridge, MA: Harvard University Press.

Halliday, M.A.K., & Hasan, R. (1989). *Language, context, and text: Aspects of language in a social-semiotic perspective.* New York: Oxford University Press.

Kinneavy, J. (1971). *A theory of discourse.* New York: W.W. Norton.

Newkirk, T. (1989). *More than stories: The range of children's writings.* Portsmouth, NH: Heinemann.

Taylor, D. (1983). *Family literacy: Young children learning to read and write.* Portsmouth, NH: Heinemann.

Vygotsky, L. (1978). *Mind in society.* Cambridge, MA: Harvard University Press.

Wells, G., & Chang-Wells, G.L. (1992). *Constructing knowledge together: Classrooms as centers of inquiry and literacy.* Portsmouth, NH: Heinemann.

Choose-your-own writing

Dian G. Smith

Volume 49, Number 5, February 1996

"...and then...and then...and then..." Do you recognize the rhythm of the third- or fourth-grade story? As a writing teacher, you can fight it—teach story structure, insist on a plot mountain that slopes down to a denouement—or you can give up sometimes and go with what seems to be the developmentally appropriate flow. One traditional way to go with this flow is to teach a unit on the "tall tale," a classic story form that suits the writing style of accumulation. Read stories about Paul Bunyan to the children and then let them create their own outsized heroes and heroines who fight bears, swallow rivers, swim oceans, and then...and then...and then....

But if you want to win young hearts and minds and perhaps hook a few reluctant readers at the same time, consider basing a unit on the popular Choose-Your-Own Adventure (Bantam) or Twist-a-Plot book series. These books may not be an advanced form of literature, but they have many advantages as a writing project. The project can be done by a group while respecting individuality. One of these books can be used as a model for discovering that books have structure; its short segments are the perfect size for teaching

constructive criticism and many aspects of editing without requiring overwhelming amounts of revision. The end product is enviable and universally gratifying.

For reluctant readers, this project has the added advantage of introducing a particularly accessible genre of literature, which may provide the satisfaction or practice that will draw them into books. (I believe that any reading is good reading so long as it brings pleasure and is not done solely from a screen.)

My Choose-Your-Own (CYO) adventure lesson was taught to five children in a resource room, but it could be applied easily to a classroom with the children divided into groups of four or five.

Writing CYO stories. First, the children need to discover the structure of a CYO story. Find a model from the simpler, shorter series. Read the introduction aloud which will explain that the reader gets to make choices about what happens as the story progresses. Then begin reading the story aloud until you reach the first choice point indicated by two lines of instructions at the bottom of the page such as these:

If you want to fight the thrashing, frothing monster, turn to page 6.

If you want to run and hide in a dark, stinky tunnel, turn to page 8.

Have one child read these lines, then pass the book to the next child (or a designated reader in the next group) who will turn to page 6 or 8 and read the instructions at the bottom of that page, and so on. These descriptions of choices will give the children an idea of how such a story progresses.

Meanwhile, as they read, map the structure of the book on the board. Figure 1, for example, is a map of *The Green Slime* (Saunders, Bantam, 1982), which I used. The numbers are page numbers and endings have been circled. (The numbers missing from the sequence are illustration pages.)

Discuss the structure, emphasizing that the children will probably want to write fewer pages. Figure 2 with 7 choice points, 8 endings, and 16 pages, represents a good length unless you have some very prolific writers.

Be flexible. When the children start writing, they may decide that they want to have some pages that do not offer a choice or that two story lines should converge, as in the professional model. My group did both.

Figure 1
Map of the structure of <u>The Green Slime</u>, using page numbers
(endings are circled)

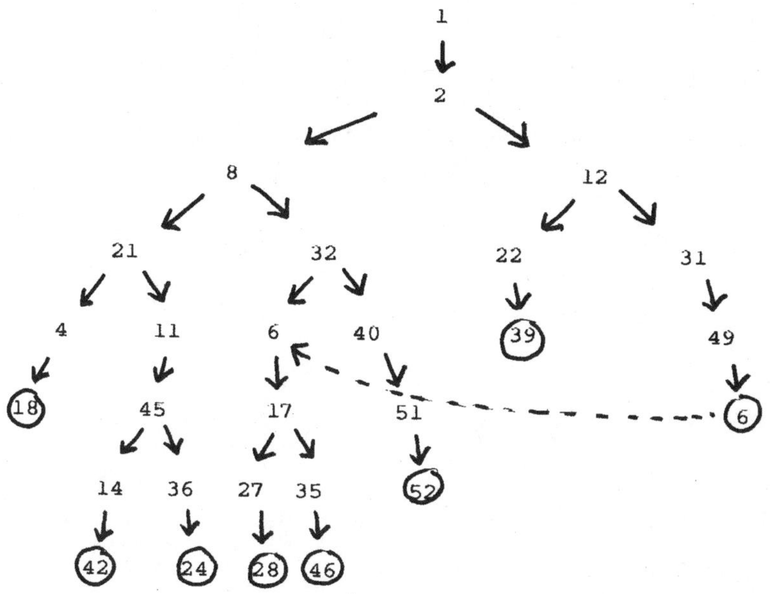

Each group then brainstorms to agree on a character, an initial setting, and the first set of choices. My group decided that "you" are at your birthday party and are offered two gifts (the first choice), which then leads to choices to visit the past or the future.

Now the group is ready to begin writing. One child can write page 1, the introductory description of how a CYO works, like the one you read them. Another can write page 2, describing the setting and the first set of choices. Two others can begin the two story lines. Because of absences or different work paces or the vagaries of a muse, there may be too few writing assignments at times. Since the pages tend to be short, however, this shouldn't be a problem for the full session. While they are waiting, the children not currently writing can make illustrations, map the story so far, plan ahead, or generate a list of titles.

Organizational notes. Each book page should be numbered and written or typed on a separate sheet of paper, even if the page is very short. Children could also write on large index cards (5" × 8") as some professional writers in this genre do.

It is critical that the children keep an up-to-date map of their story as it progresses. They like to have page numbers jump around, which is fine, but they need to make sure that the pages are numbered, the numbers are indicated on the map, and no numbers in the sequence are omitted.

Before writing an installment, especially at a new session, each child should reread her/his story line up to that point.

When a draft of the book is completed, the children should alternate reading aloud the different story lines to the group

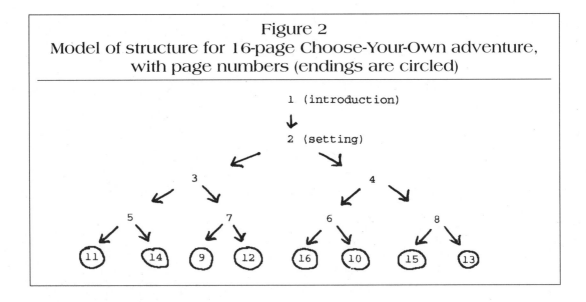

Figure 2
Model of structure for 16-page Choose-Your-Own adventure, with page numbers (endings are circled)

in order to identify needed revisions. Here are some editorial questions for them to discuss after each page:

- Does this installment make sense? Is it consistent with the preceding pages?
- Are the details and descriptions as interesting as they can be? Could something be added to make this page more exciting? (Remember, this is supposed to be an *adventure*).
- Are the sentences complete?

Now it is time to choose a title, if the children have not already done so. To give them a jump-start, discuss three different types of titles: (a) a *summary* title is like a newspaper headline, giving as much information as possible ("Terrorist Bomb Explodes at Cincinnati Airport"); (b) a *preview* title introduces the subject but in less detail ("Airport Bombing"); (c) a *teasing* title is ambiguous but catches the reader's attention ("BOOM!"). Ask the children to think of titles in these categories. Once they have a list, if there is no clear favorite, they will have to agree on a way to choose one.

Editing for capitalization, punctuation, and misspelling should be saved for a final draft according to whatever system and standards you apply.

The final copy of each page should be on a separate piece of paper. The process of book publishing depends on your resources and ingenuity. Children are usually happy with whatever form of binding you can engineer (a staple in the corner, a colored folder, or lamination) as long as they all get their own copies.

Writing to music

Linda George Scott

VOLUME 50, NUMBER 2, OCTOBER 1996

Fourth-grade students often hate writing, but they enjoy listening to music. Combining writing and music may be an effective way for teachers to unite two creative mediums. Students not only expand their appreciation for music, but they also use their writing skills and are made aware of the possibilities that exist for words and music. Creativity, imaginative thinking, music appreciation, and improved writing skills are some of the benefits that result.

I gathered several instrumental tapes for use in my classroom. Among them were tapes by modern composers and performers, some classical music, and soundtracks to popular movies. During homeroom the music played softly in the background. I first noticed how calm, quiet, and curious the children were.

We discussed the music, talking about how it made them feel, what they thought about hearing music at school, and whether or not they found that type of music pleasant. They loved it, even though it was different from the music they usually heard on the local radio stations.

The next time I used music in class, I played movie-theme music in order to re-mind my students of a familiar story. We discussed the music and watched portions of the movie to decide whether or not the music truly fit the simultaneous action. This created a great deal of interest and a lively conversation about music, words, and actions.

On another occasion we listened to instrumental music, and we wrote a story to go along with the music. I played the song a couple of times, and as students brainstormed I wrote their phrases and words on the board. Afterwards, we created a class story. When we completed it, I played the music softly while reading the story aloud. Students tried to determine whether or not the two genuinely meshed.

During the following session, I played five instrumental songs. The students were already divided into five learning groups, and each group chose one of the songs. I borrowed listening centers from the library and other teachers so that the groups could listen to their music in privacy. As they listened to their songs, they wrote words and phrases that came to mind. afterwards, they put them together and formed a story. Everyone in the class wrote a story. Students could also write a story as a group.

The students edited and then read their stories while their chosen song played softly in the background. The class loved this project. Music that they thought was for "old people" turned out to be very enjoyable for them as well.

I asked a musical composer from a local university to visit our classroom after we completed our project. He played his own music for the class, and they were full of questions. He let them write to one of his compositions, and their ability to combine words with music was amazing.

This proved to be quite a successful writing project in my classroom. Incorporating musical imagery with creative composition resulted in some inspired writing.

Beyond the classroom: Publishing student work in magazines

Karen Bromley
Diane Mannix

VOLUME 47, NUMBER 1, SEPTEMBER 1993

Publishing student writing in the classroom is an event that occurs frequently in many schools. Publishing makes the reading-writing connection real as it engages students in the writing process and the communication of meaning to a real audience. The opportunity to publish one's work for others to see, touch, read, and reread has special appeal and provides many students with an incentive to write.

Within the classroom and school, written work can be read orally or posted on bulletin boards and in hallways, printed in class and school newsletters, and shared in books that are created in writing centers. But what about publishing student work beyond the classroom? Calkins and Harwayne (1991) strongly endorse publishing for other audiences: "Teachers...would be wise to devote less time to mounting children's writing into bulletin boards and more time to helping children find real-world audiences for their writing" (p. 111). When

students write for audiences other than the teacher or their peers, they broaden their literacy perspectives by reading and writing on a wide range of topics and in varied formats, and they engage in the process of real-world writing and publishing.

We found 36 student magazines at various grade levels that provide one avenue for publishing beyond the classroom. We used three sources to obtain our information: *Magazines for Young People* (Katz & Katz, 1991), *Magazines for Children* (Stoll, 1990), and *The Standard Periodical Directory* (Manning, 1990). The Table provides magazine names, grade levels, focuses, and types of student work published. The Bibliography contains magazine descriptions with addresses for subscriptions and submission of student work. (When two addresses appear, the first is for copies and subscriptions and the second is for student work.)

These magazines publish student writing on such specific topics as the environment, science and technology, nature, health and nutrition, history, consumer issues, space and astronomy, as well as general interest articles. Original drawings and photographs, book reviews, contest responses, personal opinion essays, creative fiction including stories and plays, descriptions of crafts and hobbies, jokes and riddles, letters, poems, questions, and true stories are printed.

Several magazines are notable because they have a special focus. *Children's Album*, *Creative Kids*, *Merlyn's Pen*, *Prism*, *Shoe Tree*, and *Stone Soup* are literary magazines devoted exclusively to the publication of distinguished student writing. *Daybreak Star*, written by Native Americans, features Native American life around the U.S. Both *Faces: The Magazine About People* and *National Geographic World* have a multicultural focus and feature children and people from around the world. *Wee Wisdom* and *Boys' Life* are available in Braille for students with visual impairments. *Zillions* publishes VCR reviews. *Chart Your Course!*, *Free Spirit: News and Views on Growing Up*, and *Prism* are aimed at gifted and talented students.

Actually reading a magazine will give students an immediate sense of what gets published and how other students' work looks. You can obtain magazines from your school or public library or by writing a letter requesting a complimentary copy. Most publishers eagerly oblige, usually sending a sample volume and sometimes copies for an entire class.

Bibliography of magazines for publishing student writing

Bear Essential News for Kids. 2406 S. 24 St., Phoenix, AZ 85034, USA.

Distributed without charge to children in Arizona, California, and Georgia. Advertises products and services of interest to families.

Boys' Life. 1325 Walnut Hill Lane, PO Box 152079, Irving, TX, 75015-2079, USA; Braille ed.: Volunteer Services for the Blind, 919 Walnut St., Philadelphia, PA 19107, USA.

Published by the Boy Scouts of America. Features articles about hobbies, sports, scouting, the dangers of drugs, science, careers, and adventure, as well as fiction and comics.

Chart Your Course! PO Box 6448, Mobile, AL, 36660, USA.

Magazine published by and for gifted, creative, and talented children. Includes prose, poetry, reviews, essays, puzzles, games, art, photos, comics, and letters.

Chickadee. 255 Great Arrow Ave., Buffalo, NY 14207, USA.

A "see and do" magazine with animal stories, crafts, photographs, games, posters, and experiments.

Child Life. Children's Better Health Institute, 1100 Waterway Blvd., PO Box 567, Indianapolis, IN 46206, USA.

Health tips, recipes, a doctor's column, stories, and informative articles are the core of this magazine. Also included are puzzles and games.

Children's Album. 1320 Galaxy Way, Concord, CA 94520, USA.

Features creative writing, arts, and crafts.

Children's Digest. Children's Better Health Institute, 1100 Waterway Blvd., PO Box 567, Indianapolis, IN 46206, USA.

Presents articles on health, fiction, nonfiction, poems, cartoons, puzzles, recipes, and games for preteens.

Children's Playmate. Children's Better Health Institute, 1100 Waterway Blvd., PO Box 567, Indianapolis, IN 46206, USA.

Teaches children about health and the value of good nutrition and exercise. Each issue includes recipes, articles, puzzles, stories, poetry, games, riddles, and jokes.

Cobblestone: The History Magazine for Young People. 30 Grove St., Peterborough, NH 03458, USA.

A theme-related magazine containing stories, games, songs, articles, contests, maps, cartoons, poems, and recipes to encourage interest in and involvement with American history.

Creative Kids. PO Box 637, 100 Pine Ave., Holmes, PA 19043, USA; PO Box 6448, 350 Weinacker Ave., Mobile, AL 36660-0448, USA.

This award-winning magazine presents stories, poetry. limericks, activities, reviews, crafts, artwork, music, cartoons, puzzles, and photography by kids for kids.

Cricket: The Magazine for Children. Box 51145, Boulder, CO 80323-1145, USA; PO Box 300, Peru, IL 61354, USA.

Offers stories and pictures from all over the world to stimulate children's imaginations. Presents fantasy, history, science, adventure, and humor in articles, stories, poems, and puzzles.

Daybreak Star: The Herb of Understanding. United Indians of All Tribes Foundation, PO Box 99100, Seattle, WA 98199, USA.

Written and edited by Native American students and adults. Each issues includes legends, drawings, and articles on housing, food, and clothing from a different geographical area.

Faces: The Magazine about People. 30 Grove St., Peterborough, NJ 03458, USA.

A theme-related anthropology magazine including articles, photographs, folk tales, activities, and book and movie recommendations.

Free Spirit: News and Views on Growing Up. 123 N. Third St., Minneapolis, MN 55401, USA.

A bimonthly magazine geared to bright and talented young people. Features topics such as friendship, goals, relationships with teachers and parents, and dealing with pressure.

Highlights for Children. PO Box 269, Columbus, OH 43272-0002; 910 Church St., Honesdale, PA 18431, USA.

Includes factual articles, short stories, crafts, cartoons, riddles, puzzles, and word games.

Hopscotch. Box 164, Bluffton, OH 45817-0164, USA.

Subtitled "The Magazine for Young Girls," it includes feature stories, biographical sketches, games, poems, and puzzles.

Humpty Dumpty's Magazine. Children's Better Health Institute, 1100 Waterway Blvd., PO Box 567, Indianapolis, IN 46206, USA.

Contains health articles, stories, poems, recipes, and activity pages.

Jack and Jill. Children's Better Health Institute, 1100 Waterway Blvd., PO 567, Indianapolis, IN 46206, USA.

Focus is good health. Includes stories, recipes, games, and puzzles.

Kid City. PO Box 51277, Boulder, CO 80322-1277, USA; One Lincoln Plaza, New York, NY 10023, USA.

Each issue follows a theme such as school, pets, movies, etc., and includes games, contests, puzzles, and cartoons.

Kidlife and Times. PO Box D, Bellport, NY 11713, USA.

Features stories and articles that encourage the reader to use imagination and reading skills.

Merlyn's Pen, The National Magazine of Student Writing. 98 Main St., East Greenwich, RI 02818, USA.

Consists of stories, essays, poems, and plays submitted by young authors. Authors receive a personal response from the magazine within 3 weeks.

National Geographic World. 17th and M Sts N.W., Washington, DC 20036, USA.

Features color photographs, illustrations, and science articles about children around the world. Includes posters, games, puzzles, contests, and crafts.

Odyssey. 7 School St., Peterborough, NJ 03458, USA.

Focuses on space exploration and astronomy and includes articles, letters, drawings, questions, answers, and contests responses.

Owl: The Discovery Magazine for Children. 255 Great Arrow Ave., Buffalo, NY 14207, USA; 56 The Esplanade, Suite 306, Toronto, ON, Canada M5E 1A7.

Published by the Young Naturalist Foundation. A participation magazine about the environment that includes articles, photographs, puzzles, recipes, and experiments to encourage children to explore their world.

P3, The Earth-based Magazine for Kids. PO Box 52, Montgomery, VT 05470, USA.

An ecology magazine designed to educate children about protecting and saving the natural world.

Prism. Box 030464, Ft. Lauderdale, FL 33303, USA.

Geared for gifted and talented youth who seek penpals or a place to publish.

Ranger Rick. 8925 Leesburg Pike, Vienna, VA 22184-0001, USA.

Published by the National Wildlife Federation, this magazine contains color photographs, articles on nature and people helping nature, and poety. Includes crafts, riddles, and puzzles.

Magazines that publish student work

Magazine	Grade level	Focus	Type of student work published										
			Art	Book reviews	Contest responses	Essays	Creative fiction	Crafts & hobbies	Jokes & riddles	Letters	Poems	Questions	True stories
Bear Essential News for Kids	PreK–7	Consumer issues									X		
Boys' Life	2–12	Boys' life						X	X	X			X
Chart Your Course!	4–6	Gifted students	X	X		X	X	X	X	X	X		
Chickadee	PreK–3	General	X										
Child Life	3–6	Health	X						X		X	X	
Children's Album	3–8	Student writing, arts & crafts	X			X	X	X	X	X	X		X
Children's Digest	3–5	Health			X			X		X	X		
Children's Playmate	1–3	Health	X						X		X	X	
Cobblestone	4–9	History	X					X		X			
Creative Kids	K–12	Student writing	X	X		X	X	X	X		X		X
Cricket	1–6	General	X		X		X			X			X
Daybreak Star	4–8	Native American life	X			X	X				X		X

(continued)

Magazines that publish student work (continued)

Magazine	Grade level	Focus	Type of student work published										
			Art	Book reviews	Contest responses	Essays	Creative fiction	Crafts & hobbies	Jokes & riddles	Letters	Poems	Questions	True stories
Faces	4–9	Anthropology	X							X	X		
Free Spirit	5–12	Growing up & gifted				X	X					X	X
Highlights for Children	PreK–6	General	X				X		X	X	X		X
Hopscotch	3–6	Girls' life								X	X		
Humpty Dumpty's Magazine	PreK–1	Health	X									X	
Jack and Jill	1–4	Health	X						X		X	X	
Kid City	1–4	General			X				X				
Kidlife and Times	1–8	Imagination	X		X		X						
Merlyn's Pen	7–12	Student writing				X	X				X		X
National Geographic World	3–12	Children of the world	X							X			
Odyssey	3–8	Space & astronomy	X		X					X		X	
Owl	3–6	Environment			X	X			X	X			
P3	K–9	Ecology	X							X	X		

(continued)

Magazines that publish student work (continued)

Magazine	Grade level	Focus	Type of student work published										
			Art	Book reviews	Contest responses	Essays	Creative fiction	Crafts & hobbies	Jokes & riddles	Letters	Poems	Questions	True stories
Prism	5–12	Student writing & gifted				X	X				X		
Ranger Rick	1–6	Nature								X		X	
Sesame Street Magazine	PreK–8	School preparation	X										
Shoe Tree	1–9	Student writing	X	X		X	X				X		X
Sports Illustrated for Kids	3–7	Sports	X						X	X	X		
Stone Soup	1–8	Student writing	X	X			X				X		X
Surprises	PreK–6	Home activities					X						
3-2-1 Contact	3–8	Science and technology			X							X	
Turtle Magazine	PreK–K	Health	X										
Wee Wisdom	K–6	Values	X			X	X	X			X		X
Zillions	3–7	Economics		X						X		X	

Sesame Street Magazine. PO Box 55518, Boulder, CO 80322-5518, USA, One Lincoln Plaza, New York, NY 10023, USA.

Designed for preschool children, each themed issue contains activities dealing with the alphabet, counting, and prereading. Includes games, stories, and color drawings.

Shoe Tree. National Association for Young Writers, PO Box 452, Belvidere, NJ 07823, USA.

A literacy magazine devoted to the encouragement of young authors. Features stories, poems, artwork, personal narrartives, and book reviews.

Sports Illustrated for Kids. Time and Life Bldg.; Rockfeller Center, New York, NY 10020, USA.

Features professional and amateur athletes, fiction, sports tips, puzzles, posters, and activities.

Stone Soup. PO Box 83, Santa Cruz, CA 95063, USA.

A literacy magazine of students' stories, poems, artwork, and book reviews. Contains information for contributors in each issue.

Surprises. PO Box 236, Chanhassen, MN 55317, USA.

Created by two teachers to provide activities for children and parents to share at home. Includes puzzles, games, math problems, and listening exercises.

3-2-1 Contact. PO Box 53051, Boulder, CO 80322-3051, USA; One Lincoln Plaza, New York, NY 10023, USA.

Includes articles, photographs, and illustrations on science and technology topics, and contains crafts, games, activities, and contests.

Turtle Magazine for Preschool Kids. Children's Better Health Institute, 1100 Waterway Blvd., PO Box 567, Indianapolis, IN 46206, USA.

Combines fun and learning with an emphasis on health. Includes stories, poems, songs, games, and puzzles.

Wee Wisdom. Unity School of Christianity, Unity Village, MO 64065, USA.

A nondenominational magazine, also available in Braille, geared toward helping children develop values. Contains puzzles, crafts, stories, and poetry.

Zillions. PO Box 51777, Boulder, CO 80321-1777, USA; 256 Washington St., Mt. Vernon, NY 10553, USA.

A Consumer Reports for children that teaches about economics and finance and helps children made moneywise decisions. Contains articles on items children buy, tests on toys, clothing and fashion ideas, movies, and good foods.

REFERENCES

Calkins, L.M. & Harwayne, S. (1991). *Living between the lines*. Portsmouth, NH: Heinemann.

Katz, B., & Katz, L.S. (1991). *Magazine for young people*. Providence, NJ: Bowker.

Manning, M. (Ed.). (1990). *The standard periodical directory* (13th ed.). New York: Oxbridge.

Stoll, D.R. (Ed.). (1990). *Magazines for children*. Glassboro, NJ: Educational Press Association of America, and Newark, DE: International Reading Association.

Beyond the classroom: Publishing student work in newspapers

Karen Bromley
Diane Mannix

VOLUME 47, NUMBER 2, OCTOBER 1993

There are many reasons for encouraging students to look beyond the classroom for opportunities to publish their writing. When students write for a real-world audience and their work is published, writing efforts are legitimized. Motivation and incentive to write can increase. Literacy perspectives are broadened as students read, write, and think about a wide range of topics and in varied formats. Students begin to see that their ideas and writing can have an impact on others.

There are many avenues for publishing student work in the world beyond the classroom. One potential outlet for student writing is the newspaper. Student "Letters to the Editor" offer the most obvious outlet for sharing opinions on any number of local, national, and international issues or concerns. But special newspaper supplements offer many other opportunities as well.

Newspapers In Education (NIE), sponsored by the American National Publishers Association (ANPA) Foundation, is a cooperative effort of newspapers working with local schools to use the newspaper as a tool for instruction. NIE encourages and supports the publication of student writing in special newspaper supplements called youth features. In the U.S. and parts of Canada, 669 daily newspapers have organized NIE programs, and over 400 daily newspapers publish youth features (*Survey*, 1989).

The type of student writing published in these youth features varies from newspaper to newspaper (*Survey*, 1989). *Peanut Butter Press*, a monthly 12-page insert in *The Indianapolis News*, Indiana, is written "by and for kids" ages 4–7. It includes a wide range of articles: interviews with elected officials and famous athletes, written summaries of tours of businesses, poetry, fiction and nonfiction short stories, book reviews, editorial columns, mazes, and word games.

"Young Ideas" appears weekly in the *Deseret News* in Salt Lake City, Utah, and includes K–12 student contributions of poetry, stories, reports, book and movie reviews, jokes, cartoons, puzzles, and tall tales.

"Kentucky Kids" appears daily in the *Lexington Herald-Leader* and includes student drawings, poems, stories, book reviews, and jokes.

Teen Gazette, published by Phoenix Newspapers, Inc., Arizona, is written by student reporters.

"Chalk It Up!" in *The Des Moines Register* in Iowa includes question-and-answer features and contests for students.

Mindworks, published monthly by the *Star Tribune* in Minneapolis, Minnesota, includes essays of up to 300 words written by students in grades 1 through 12 on topics chosen by the features staff.

Pennywhistle Press, published by Gannett Publishing, is a national newspaper supplement for ages 4-14 that is circulated in approximately 40 newspapers in the U.S. and includes student-written news, entertainment, sports, feature stories, games, puzzles, and weekly columns for reader participation.

A pen-pal exchange program sponsored by NIE and ANPA features student-written letters and the potential of improved international understandings and relations ("International Writing Exchange," 1990). *Obmen* (the Russian for 'exchange'), published by *The Gazette* in Cedar Rapids, Iowa, features monthly translated correspondence from students ages 10–12 in Sebastopol, Russia, written to Iowa students whose writings, in turn, are translated and published in the daily newspaper *Slava Sebastapolya*. *The Times* in Trenton, New Jersey, *The Nashville Tennessean*, and newspapers and schools in cities in other Soviet republics and countries are also part of this program.

To establish an NIE program or for more information on youth features, you can write to The ANPA Foundation, Box 17407, Dulles Airport, Washington, DC 20041, USA. Information on youth features, special supplements, and NIE activities at the state/provincial level is available from the newspaper or press association located in most state/provincial capitals.

REFERENCES

International writing exchange. (1990, March/April). Update: *Newspaper in education and literacy, 16* (2), 1–8. Washington, DC: American Newspaper Association Educational Services.

Survey of newspapers in education programs. (1989). Washington, DC: American Newspaper Publishers Association Foundation and International Newspaper Marketing Association.

Student portfolios: Building self-reflection in a first-grade classroom

Lindy Vizyak

Volume 48, Number 4, December 1994/January 1995

"It is some of my best work. I Xed out words that were wrong and put other words on top. I got the right spelling for Antarctica from the globe. This is fiction and has a summary. Can I read it to you?" Comments from a third or fourth grader? Actually, Aaron is a student in my first-grade classroom. His comments, which were recorded during a portfolio conference, confirmed my belief that young children can reflect upon and evaluate their own learning.

For the past 5 years, I have been using portfolios in my classroom to document student growth and to assess performance. The process has been evolving for me and for my students. During the first 3 years, my time was spent developing a portfolio model, management system, and recording forms which fit my philosophy of assessment. However, as I researched alternative methods of assessment, I became increasingly uncomfortable with a teacher-controlled model. It did not align with current research, which stresses the impor-

tance of providing opportunities for students to participate in their assessment and to reflect on their learning.

Last year, I decided to put my research-based knowledge into practice. I provided file folders for each child to collect his/her work. Some students collected work samples; most did not. At the end of the year, in reflecting on this less-than-successful experience, I decided I had not modeled the process, demonstrated possible contents of a portfolio, or discussed reasons for selecting the contents. In addition, I had not provided time for students to work with and share their portfolios. This realization prompted my decision to provide a structure this year that would support my goal of developing collaborative assessment.

I implemented my new plan by introducing the term *portfolio* during the first week of school. To provide a clear visual model, I shared my own portfolio with the class. I had decorated the cover of an 8" × 12" manila folder with my drawing of the cover of *The True Story of the Three Pigs*

(Scieszka, 1989; a favorite children's book), a drawing of my family, and a University of Colorado logo. (My son is a recent graduate.) I also shared the contents of my portfolio and explained the significance of each entry. Children were given blank folders to decorate and then share with the class. This first step created instant ownership.

Figure 1

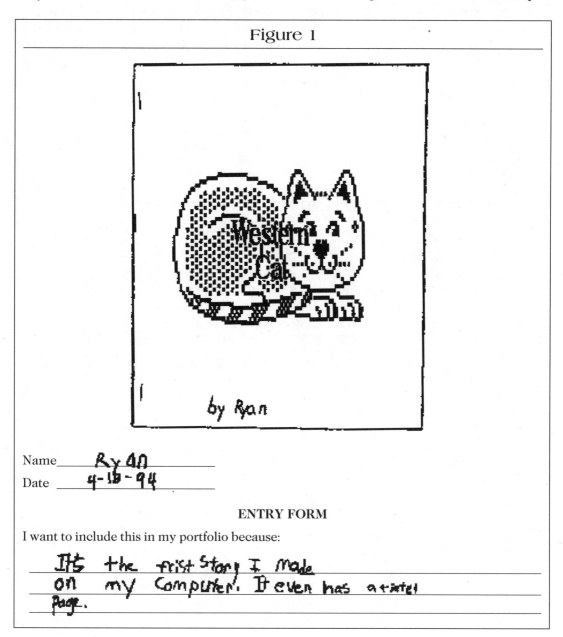

by Ryan

Name _Ryan_

Date _4-18-94_

ENTRY FORM

I want to include this in my portfolio because:

It's the frist story I made on my Computer. It even has a titel page.

Several times each week, students shared pieces from their portfolios with each other and explained the reasoning behind their selections. At the beginning of the year, students had no previous experience with this process, and most found it difficult to explain their choices. Ryan shared a story he had written about his dog and said simply, "I put this in my portfolio because it is about my dog and I like my dog."

I wanted to model other possible reasons for Ryan's including the story in his portfolio, so I said, "I know that Ryan loves to write and often writes at home and during his free time. I also see that he has a title for his story." Ryan promptly added, "Oh, yeah. I also have a summary on the

---

Figure 2

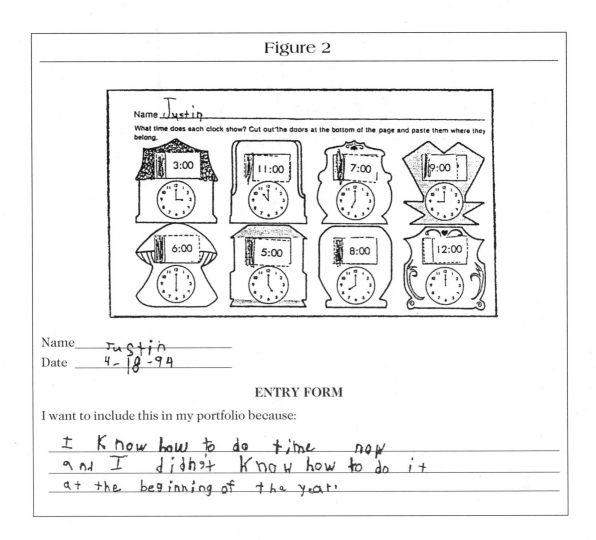

Name_Justin_

What time does each clock show? Cut out the doors at the bottom of the page and paste them where they belong.

3:00   11:00   7:00   9:00

6:00   5:00   8:00   12:00

Name___Justin___

Date___4-18-94___

ENTRY FORM

I want to include this in my portfolio because:

I Know how to do time now and I didh't Know how to do it at the beginning of the year.

---

back of my story." I asked him where he got the idea, and he said that he noticed many of the books I read to the class had a summary on the back. Ryan clearly had made a connection between reading and writing!

Drawing on my experience with writer's workshop minilessons, I structured portfolio minilessons. I focused on the content of student-managed portfolios and reasons for the selections. These lessons provided the language needed for self-reflection. The majority of the first student selections were examples of best work. As the year progressed, minilessons explored other reasons for selecting portfolio pieces: something you have learned (growth), something that took a long time (effort), something that was challenging (risk-taking), and something that showed interests outside of school (wholistic learning).

The students have generated a classroom chart that lists "Things That Can Go in a Portfolio." The list includes a story or book, science projects, letters, notes, cards, best work, math papers, artwork, photographs, things from home, challenging things, things that demonstrate improvement, and work from a favorite subject. The list is ongoing and is expanded as students discover new categories of possible portfolio inclusions.

Each Friday, anyone who has a new portfolio entry (including me) is invited to share it with the class. These regular share sessions have resulted in improved metacognition and opportunities for building self-esteem and confidence as students develop a voice in the assessment process.

In addition to the student-managed portfolio, I also have a teacher-student portfolio. Twice a month, students meet with a volunteer and choose one or two pieces from their teacher-student portfolio. They may select assessment data (reading and writing conference notes, miscues, math tasks, content-area unit tests, etc.), student work samples (story maps, responses to literature, projects, writing samples, problem solving, etc.), or parent input (surveys, conference notes, etc.). An entry form slip that explains the student's reason(s) for each choice is attached to the appropriate piece. This process gives students practice in selecting meaningful work and reflecting on those selections. It also provides valuable information for me about each student's ability to self-reflect.

Next year, I will not have an assistant in my classroom, so I have set a realistic goal to confer with each student once every 9-week grading period. I feel confident that our new teacher-student portfolio is a successful marriage of student reflection, self-evaluation, and teacher accountability.

Readers Theatre and the writing workshop: Using children's literature to prompt student writing

Loretta T. Stewart

VOLUME 51, NUMBER 2, OCTOBER 1997

The benefits of having students examine well-written pieces of literature are well established. Routman (1991) in *Invitations* says that examining texts "directs students' attention back to the text in a careful, critical manner" (p. 111). I think of it as having them "crawl" around in the text, and I find success in using good literature as models for student writing.

After reading a piece of literature, my students and I examine it together. Then I ask them to be aware of literary devices in the books they are reading. Older students are not always eager to reread, and I wanted my students to look back closely at the author's craft in *Charlotte's Web* (White, 1952). Readers Theatre provided the vehicle that carried my students back to Zuckerman's barn for a closer look.

Readers Theatre has long been a part of my reading workshop, but using this activity in a writing workshop came about by accident. It began when I found a classroom set of *Charlotte's Web*. In years past

I had used sections of this text on an overhead for classes to examine the literary devices used by E.B. White. Finding the classroom set gave me the idea to put the books into the hands of students for examination. The extensive use of dialogue in this book is perfect for teaching dialogue writing. This same rich use of dialogue makes *Charlotte's Web* an ideal choice for Readers Theatre. Furthermore, it offers a variety of writing topics that students can explore.

Readers Theatre

Routman (1991) defines Readers Theatre as "creating a script from a narrative text and performing it for an audience" (p. 98). I like to find sections or chapters of books, have students take the various character parts, and ask them to read directly from the text. I ask students not to mark the text, but rather to follow along and use the conventions of punctuation and indenting as signposts to direct their reading. This type of reading offers wonderful support for below-level readers.

The day I passed out the books to a noisy chorus of, "I've seen the movie," I explained that because we already knew what was going to happen to Wilbur, we could concentrate on what White did as a writer to make this book, published in 1952, still popular. I had already examined the chapters and noted that most chapters could be adapted for four readers. My students sat at tables in groups of four, and I let the groups decide how to divide the parts. The wide range of reading levels in my classroom was not a problem because Readers Theatre is a support reading activity that lends itself to using one text for the whole group.

At the beginning of each class, I explained the characters involved, and often gave students something to be aware of in the reading. For instance, I might ask them to decide if Fern could really understand what the animals were saying and to support their opinions with evidence from the text. Later in the story, Fern becomes interested in boys and loses her ability to understand the animals, which leads to an ongoing point of discussion. Some days all groups were taking character parts and reading orally from the same chapter. As groups finished, they wrote short responses in their day books and compared responses within the groups, preparing to discuss with the whole class.

If the chapter included many characters the whole class did Readers Theatre as a change of pace. Chapters that had more narration than dialogue gave us a chance to listen to E.B. White read on tape. Students enjoyed the variety of small-group or whole-class Readers Theatre, listening to chapters on tape, and lively discussions. Our close examination of this book offered a wealth of examples of character development, evidence of author research, and story structure.

Literary devices

Each day after the readings, we examined the following literary devices used by White:

Lists.

> ...all sorts of things that you find in barns: ladders, grindstones, pitch forks, monkey wrenches, scythes, lawn mowers, snow shovels, ax handles, milk pails, water buckets, empty grain sacks, and rusty rat traps. (p. 14)

Foreshadowing.

> ...she had a kind heart, and she was to prove loyal and true to the very end. (p. 41)

Rich sensory descriptions.

> Wilbur amused himself in the mud along the edge of the brook, where it was warm and moist and delightfully sticky and oozy. (pp. 10–11)

> There were lights on the midway, and you could hear the crackle of the gambling machines and the music of the merry-go-round and the voice of the man in the beano booth calling numbers. (p. 138)

Humor (subtle to slapstick).

> "Can I have a pig, too, Pop?" asked Avery. "No, I only distribute pigs to early risers," said Mr. Arable. "Fern was up at daylight,

trying to rid the world of injustice. As a result, she now has a pig. It just shows what can happen if a person gets out of bed promptly." (p. 5)

Alliterative sound play.

"In a forest looking for beechnuts and truffles and delectable roots, pushing leaves aside with my wonderful strong nose, searching and sniffing along the ground, smelling, smelling, smelling...." (p. 61)

The daily discussions of literary devices, characterization, and story structure sparked ideas for students' writing. We brainstormed topics and came up with ideas such as character changes, the stereotyping of Avery, the role of seasons, effective literary devices, and a comparison of literary devices used in *Charlotte's Web* to those White used in *The Trumpet of the Swan* (1970) or *Stuart Little* (1945). Several students chose to research spiders or the life of White.

Students webbed ideas and, using the book, found quotes to support their ideas. A minilesson helped students understand how to use and punctuate quotations. Students crawled around in the text of *Charlotte's Web*, finding support for their writing topics. Rough drafts were shared, feedback given, revisions made, second drafts edited, and final drafts written.

As a writing model

Charlotte's Web was an excellent text for working on dialogue in student writing. E.B. White was a master at using dialogue to move the story action along. Students' close attention to the conventions of dialogue required in Readers Theatre carried over to their own writing. Minilessons on using the conventions for writing dialogue enabled my students to catch on much faster. We examined and discussed overheads I had created that demonstrated the importance of format and punctuation. A sample of the first overhead follows. I used the dialogue on the first page of the story, minus the formatting and conventions for dialogue.

> Where's Papa going with that ax? Out to the hoghouse. Some pigs were born last night. I don't see why he needs an ax. Well, one of the pigs is a runt. It's very small and weak and it will never amount to anything. So your father has decided to do away with it. Do away with it? You mean kill it? Just because it is smaller than the others? (p. 1)

We discussed the difficulty of understanding who was talking in this example. Several students tried using Readers Theatre and found it confusing. Then we compared it with the following example using the same text, but with indents to cue speakers.

> Where's Papa going with that ax?
>> Out to the hoghouse. Some pigs were born last night.
>> I don't see why he needs an ax.
>> Well, one of the pigs is a runt. It's very small and weak, and it will never amount to anything. So your father has decided to do away with it.
>> Do away with it? You mean kill it? Just because it's smaller than the others? (p. 1)

We talked about how indenting works as a cue for a new speaker, and we decided it was still difficult to feel involved with the dialogue because we didn't know enough about the speakers and their relationships. The last overhead showed how adding the descriptive information makes punctuation necessary.

> "Where's Papa going with that ax?" said Fern to her mother as they were setting the table for breakfast.
> "Out to the hoghouse," replied Mrs. Arable. "Some pigs were born last night."
> "I don't see why he needs an ax," continued Fern, who was only eight.
> "Well," said her mother, "one of the pigs is a runt. It's very small and weak, and it will never amount to anything. So your father has decided to do away with it."
> "Do away with it?" shrieked Fern. "You mean kill it? Just because it's smaller than the others?"

With the addition of descriptive information regarding the speakers, students agreed that punctuation was necessary to separate the spoken words from the description. The students' involvement in Readers Theatre made the explanation much more meaningful.

I was delighted to find an improvement in their use of written dialogue. This example from a piece by Elise shows her use of dialogue and description.

> Suddenly our car sputtered out of gas.
> "Oh, great! Mom, did you check the gas before we left?" I asked.
> "No, Honey, I forgot. There's a little town over there." She nodded toward distant lights. "Maybe I can get help there. Wait here until I get back." She opened the door and got out of our van.

Another example from a story by Joelle:

> "Why have you come?" she demanded. She stood dark and mysterious against the dusk sky.
> Shagrat's lips curled. He sneered and laughed. "Go woman! There is nothing you can do for your people now!"

The student writing that evolved from this experience was evidence enough for me that sixth graders' writing was enhanced by studying writers like E.B. White. A good piece of literature can extend an invitation to write and be used as a model for writing. Using Readers Theatre allowed us to revisit *Charlotte's Web*, reread a familiar piece of text in an interesting way, and examine the author's craft more closely. Requiring students to document their statements with evidence from the text sent them crawling around in a book that has been popular with young people for 45 years. The experience of using Readers Theatre to initiate this examination of text and to prompt writing could be used with other selections as well. There are many books at all reading levels that offer rich literature to explore with Readers Theatre.

REFERENCES

Neumeyer, P.F. (1994). *The annotated Charlotte's Web*. New York: HarperCollins.

Routman, R. (1991). *Invitations: Changing as teachers and learners K–12*. Portsmouth, NH: Heinemann.

White, E.B. (1945). *Stuart Little*. New York: Harper & Row.

White, E.B. (1952). *Charlotte's web*. New York: Harper & Row.

White, E.B. (1970). *The trumpet of the swan*. New York: Harper & Row.

White, E.B. (Speaker). (1970). *Charlotte's web* (Cassette Recording). New York: Bantam Audio Publishing.

Students as authors

Anita Rinehart Nedeff
Nancy Brady
Barbara Maxwell
Ruth Oaks
Mary Anne Seckel

VOLUME 47, NUMBER 4, DECEMBER 1993/JANUARY 1994

The Students as Authors Project, established in 1991, is a school-wide project that entails writing, illustrating, and publishing books of all genres *by* children *for* children. These books are written in English, several other languages, and sign language. Our 49 ESL (English as a Second Language) students and their parents help with translations of the books.

After classroom lessons in consumer education, the intermediate students at Central Elementary School set the operating standards for the project. Cost effectiveness was a prime consideration. As a result of their studies, the students established a publishing company. In May 1991, a schoolwide contest was held to choose a name and logo. Overwhelmingly, the children selected the entry of Sally Zhang, a fifth grade student from China. Central's WORM Publishing Company had its beginning. WORM is an acronym

for *Worlds of a Readers Mind.* The winning student explained that one is never limited in books. The mind can travel anywhere. A sketch of the logo shows a worm crawling out of a book with the slogan "We crawl into good books."

173

After books are published they are sold to families and community members and at school functions. Single copies of each selection are displayed at school. Since the project has been so successful, the third-grade class has opened a student-operated school store where new selections of the month are available with best-selling selections of previous months.

Every child at Central Elementary School writes books at school as single authors, with partners, in small groups, or as entire classes, according to the goals of the grade level. Generally, the books evolve during cooperative, integrated classroom instruction. The Chapter 1 Reading Specialist works with classroom teachers to deliver this instruction; she also directs the Students as Authors Project and is responsible for its ongoing operation.

As the stories are completed, the editing process begins. The Chapter 1 Reading Specialist models the editing process for the entire class; then she provides a writing checklist for self-editing, peer editing, and teacher/author conferencing. The stories are recopied by hand, word processed, or typed. Finally, the authors illustrate them to prepare for publication. The original of each book is color copied in multiple copies with the original stored for further use. The authors and parents agree that for US$3.50 and a copy of the book for their collections, WORM may purchase the rights to their stories solely for the purpose of reproducing and selling the books to earn money to keep the project self-generating.

After the second year of the project we have

- sold several hundred books to parents, interested people in the community, public school teachers, and teachers in higher education,
- managed to balance our accounts at the end of each year,
- received in-kind contributions from several businesses and families and friends of Central Elementary School,
- shown an increase in students' self-esteem as determined by our Self-Esteem Survey,
- received requests to expand the project to other schools in our county and outside the state,
- received requests to provide inservice of other faculties,
- received requests to provide written materials to share with other schools.

The Students as Authors Project has benefited all students, our school, and all teachers who have participated during the past 2 years. As we begin our third year of the project our children will continue their improvement in reading comprehension, process writing, critical thinking skills, and increasing self-esteem. Children in other schools will benefit from the implementation of this project as we aid their faculties in establishing goals to meet their needs.

Nancie, you lied! With special thanks to Nancie Atwell

Dianne Dodsworth

VOLUME 47, NUMBER 6, MARCH 1994

I read your book from cover to cover. I put bookmarks in all the special places until *In the Middle* (Atwell, 1987) resembled a well-worn and revered Bible. I underlined and highlighted. I was ready to face 24 fresh-faced, eager Grade 4s. I opened the book to Chapter 4, "Getting Started," and pushed the "on" button. It was going to be a great year. After all, wasn't it clear—a minilesson here, a status of the class conference there. All I'd have to do is flip to the minilesson marker and follow the directions—like following a cookbook, only, in this case, I "feed the mind"!

But, Nancie, you lied! You gave me very explicit directions about getting started. You told me that "On the first day, I lay the foundation of this structure." I believed you. I thought that if I echoed your words that my kids would do as yours did. But they didn't. I put my head down and started to write. I didn't look up. I didn't watch to see who was writing and who wasn't. I was busy; I did mean business and my posture demonstrated that. I was expecting everyone else to become a writer and join me.

I looked up. Some little heads were bent over but most were sitting there staring at me. Hadn't these children ever seen a teacher writing before? From the looks on their faces I could see that this was all new to them. Now what? Quick, check the marker for Topic Conferences. "Tell me about your neighborhood..." Finally, a few more heads went down until, in one way or another, there was a symbolic representation of what I imagined your classroom, Nancie, might look like.

So we limped and worked our way through the days and weeks. We were doing it! The Writing Workshop was underway! I still marveled at your athletic ability and stamina. Anyone who could manage a 5-minute minilesson, a quick, 5-minute status of the class check, writing workshop and 5–10 minute class conference must be in top physical and mental condition, honed to split second precision. At this rate, we'll be so efficient that the program will have no choice but to succeed.

But Nancie, you lied! We weren't able to keep up. Our minilessons often spilt over into recess. On some days we didn't even get to write! The status of the class check seemed to go on forever. I just couldn't bear to cut off Sarah when she begged to tell me about her new puppy. As for the 5–10 minute class conference, forget it. We got so wrapped up in all our stories that often we went right through recess!

So, what to do? We all walked the line between the carefully laid out formula—guaranteed to succeed—and the somewhat hazy world of what was turned out to be a laid-back writing workshop. Some days we wrote for an hour, others we talked, on others we "walked" each other through some tricky editing concerns. Did you really try to trick us, Nancie? Was this your way of showing us what happens when we jump on the bandwagon and walk in someone else's shoes? Whatever your hidden message, you certainly fooled us. We thought your way was the only way. Were we wrong!

Now, Nancie, let me tell you what really worked.

A year later, I realized that nobody else's approach can work in my classroom. We all simply work in different ways. I had to find this out for myself. Now I set my agenda and work from that framework. We read, we share, we respond, we write, we confer, and we meet as a large group. I keep the framework simple, but so much happened within it! Knowing what I know now about coming to meaning, I simply can't lock step my way there and neither can my students.

So, Nancie, what does my classroom look like now? My writing workshop has a form of minilesson, a form of status of the class check, and a form of class conference but they float around within the workshop format and don't resemble what I grabbed onto so quickly and fervently. They surface as needed and are only tools to help us as we negotiate and confer our way through the writing process.

Don't get me wrong, Nancie. This is not a wishy-washy unstructured program. The difference is that the structure is mine and is open for negotiation if it doesn't work.

> Looking to myself
> Looking to my kids
> Only we can decide
> What works for us
>
> It takes awhile
> With lots of thought
> To realize that...
>
>   By...
> Looking to myself
> Looking to my kids
> Only we can decide.

REFERENCE

Atwell, N. (1987). *In the middle*. Portsmouth, NH: Heinemann.

Enhancing reading and writing through competitions

Frances A. Karnes
Tracy L. Riley

VOLUME 51, NUMBER 3, NOVEMBER 1997

Competitions that develop and enhance skills in reading and writing are many and varied. Some focus on creative writing, others on literature, and still others on the skills of readers and writers in a wide array of contexts. Increasing the availability of contests, quiz bowls, and the like gives balance to the sports and athletic events conducted in the schools (Zirkes & Penna, 1984). A stronger sense of pride for both the school and community also develops as students are recognized and rewarded for participation in such competitions (Williams, 1986). A sampling of competitions that will excite and motivate students in reading and writing follows.

Students of all ages will enjoy *We Are Writers, Too!*, a contest that provides young people with an outlet for publication of their original written works. Poetry and prose writing are accepted for possible publication on the basis of creativity, research, and, of course, originality. Up to 100 writings are published each year. For more details, contact Creative With Words Publications, PO Box 223226, Carmel, CA 93922, USA.

Those young Shakespeares of the 1990s will be inspired by the *Young Playwrights Festival*. The competition is open to all playwrights under the age of 18 and encourages self-expression through playwriting. Each playwright receives a written evaluation of the work submitted—and the winning play is produced in the Young Playwrights Festival in New York City. What a wonderful experience for a young person to be able to participate in the casting, rehearsal, and production of his or her own play! Write to Young Playwrights Inc., 321 West 44th Street, Suite 906, New York, NY 10036, USA, for further information.

Writers between the ages of 6 and 19 will find *The National Written and Illustrated by... Awards Contest for Students* both fun and challenging. The contest inspires and motivates students to write, illustrate, and assemble original books using their creativity and talent. Reading can be enhanced also as student winners have their books published for others to enjoy. Selected authors are invited to Kansas City, Missouri, USA, where the staff of Landmark publications assists in the final production phases for the published books. Royalties are paid annually on the sales of the books. If this sounds like something of interest to your class, write to Landmark Editions Inc., PO Box 4469, Kansas City, MO 64217, USA.

Authors can find out more about what their readers think and feel from students who participate in the *Letters About Literature Essay Contest*. Students in Grades 6–10 select a book they have recently read, and write a letter (addressed to the author) about how the book made them feel. Winners receive an expenses-paid trip to Washington, D.C. to attend a special luncheon at the Library of Congress. For additional details write to Read Magazine, The Weekly Reader, 245 Long Hill Road, Middletown, CT 06457-9291, USA.

If reading the newspaper and staying current on national and world events are goals of your school's reading program, check out the *Annual NewsCurrents Student Editorial Cartoon Contest* (open to students of all ages). Students use their reading and comprehension skills to create editorial cartoons. And for such cartoons to make a point, you've got to know your stuff! The outstanding cartoonists are awarded savings bonds, as well as publication of their cartoons. Write for further details to the Annual NewsCurrents Student Editorial Cartoon Contest, Knowledge Unlimited, Inc., PO Box 52, Madison, WI 53701, USA.

Recognize students for reading goals set in individual classrooms through use of *Pizza Hut's BOOK IT! National Reading Incentive Program*. Classroom teachers establish reading goals and kids win prizes, including buttons, stickers, and pizza. Goals may relate to the number of books read, number of chapters or pages read, number of minutes spent reading, or any other appropriate reading objective suitable for the curriculum. If all of the class meets the reading goal for 4 of the 5 months, the class receives a pizza party. For more information contact your local Pizza Hut manager or write to Pizza Hut, BOOK IT!, PO Box 2999, Wichita, KS 67201, USA.

Middle school students interested in the Holocaust can reflect upon the topic and its implication in our lives today by participating in the *National Writing and Art Contest on the Holocaust*. Students submit poems, newspaper articles, stories, plays, essays, or research papers reflecting their views and understanding related to the Holocaust. Judging is based upon originality, content, quality of expression, and historical accuracy, with winners recognized at a ceremony in Washington, D.C. at the United States Holocaust Memorial Museum. Contact the United States Holocaust Memorial Museum, 100 Raoul Wallenberg Place S.W., Washington, DC 20021-2150, USA, Attention: National Writing and Art Contest.

Several additional student magazines offer an assortment of contests and competitions in reading and writing. Teachers should check *Merlyn's Pen, Read, Cricket,* and other similar magazines for details. The variety of opportunities these publications give students is amazing.

A few tips from sponsors of reading and writing competitions are given by Karnes and Riley (1996a) as follows:

1. Students should be certain to read guidelines carefully. One competition, for example, will not accept products that have been written for classroom assignments. Another competition will not accept entries that are placed in decorative folders. These minor details are quite important and may determine how well a child competes...or even if the opportunity for competition is given.

2. Students' writing should reflect who they are as individuals. Several competitions are clearly based upon the concepts that students have their own ideas and that those ideas are valued. In such a case, students should be encouraged to be "honest, personal, and conversational" (Karnes & Riley, 1996a, p. 56).

3. Students need to look and plan ahead. For example, the National Council of Teachers of English advises students to begin planning for participation in competitions at least 1 year in advance of their grade eligibility.

4. Students should be certain to photocopy or save their entries on computer disk. Some competition sponsors clearly state that entries are not returned.

Additionally, students should determine participation early in order to allow time for completion if special materials are needed (Karnes & Riley, 1996a). Precision is also vital. "Mistakes such as typographical errors, misspelled words, inaccurate calculations, and size requirement deviations may count against the applicant" (Karnes & Riley, 1996b, p. 49). Of course there are other tips and techniques that each teacher will incorporate in individual classrooms with particular students participating in specific competitions.

Participation in competitions can take place in the classroom or outside of the school environment. However, it doesn't have to be an activity that is isolated from the curriculum and seemingly irrelevant to the classroom. We have designed a Competitions Journal, which provides students an avenue for further thought and discussion (Karnes & Riley, 1996a). Within the journal students are asked to brainstorm why they want to participate in competitions, to select their top 10 competitions, and to set competition goals. Furthermore, students are given examples of letters to sponsors, as well as some time management tips. Self-evaluation also comes into play as students begin to consider their performance in regard to planning, organization, time management, participation, and products. These are but a few examples of meaningful ways that language arts teachers can incorporate competitions into the classroom.

Perhaps the most important aspect of participating in competitions is the recognition both students and teachers receive. It is important that students are perceived by themselves and others as winners simply because they have participated in reading and writing competitions. Teachers, parents, and administrators should recognize the efforts of students as they take the risks competitions offer. Through the efforts and enthusiasm of reading teachers involving their students in reading and writing competitions, the pace is set for every student to demonstrate and expand his or her abilities.

REFERENCES

Karnes, F.A., & Riley, T.L. (1996a). *Competitions: Maximizing your abilities*. Waco, TX: Prufrock Press.

Karnes, F.A., & Riley, T.L. (1996b). Competitions developing and nurturing talents. *Gifted Child Today, 19* (2), 14–15, 47–50.

Williams, A.T. (1986). Academic game bowls as a teaching/learning tool. *Gifted Child Today, 9* (1), 2–5.

Zirkes, M., & Penna, R. (1984). Improving school climate with academic competitions. *NASSP-Bulletin, 68,* 94–97.

Providing books and other print materials for classroom and school libraries

A position statement of the International Reading Association

The International Reading Association calls for an immediate increase in funding for books in classroom, school, and town libraries. The condition of these libraries has weakened over the last decade; there are fewer books per child, and the condition of the books and the staffing of the libraries have seriously deteriorated. We must reverse this trend because children who have access to books are more likely to read for enjoyment, and thus increase their reading skills and their desire to read to learn. The purpose of this position statement is to emphasize the importance of increased, dedicated funding for the purchase of quality literature of multiple genres. Libraries must purchase a sufficient number of new books per student and they must make a concentrated effort to replace older materials for each classroom and school library on an annual basis. Genres should include picture storybooks, novels, biography, fiction and nonfiction material, magazines, poetry, and a multitude of other types to suit the interests and range of reading abilities of all children.

Why is it important for children to have access to books?

A strong research base supports the importance of access to books. Children who are allowed to self-select to read and who have access to varied sources of print materials in their classrooms, school libraries, town libraries, and at home, read more and read more widely, both for pleasure and for information. Children who do a substantial amount of voluntary reading demonstrate positive attitudes toward reading, and these students tend to be the best readers (Calkins, 1996; Greaney, 1980; Krashen, 1994).

Frequent reading is related to the development of sophisticated language structures, higher levels of comprehension, improved word analysis skills, and fluency.

Significant amounts of voluntary reading are associated with greater interest and skill development (Irving, 1980). In one study, kindergarten children who demonstrated a voluntary interest in books were rated by their teachers as displaying high performance in all areas of school achievement. They also performed well on a standardized achievement test (Morrow, 1983). In other studies, classrooms were filled with large numbers of trade books, and teachers were asked to encourage free reading. Improvement in children's reading achievement, gains in vocabulary and comprehension, and increased reading were noted, and better attitudes toward reading were reported than were exhibited by children in comparison schools who did not participate in such programs (Elley & Mangubhai, 1983; Fielding, Wilson, & Anderson, 1986; Ingham, 1981).

What does "access to books" mean?

Access to books refers to the availability of quality literature in classroom, school, community, or home libraries. Children with adequate access to books have many books to select from on a daily basis, both in and out of school. Additionally, school libraries and classrooms must have an adequate amount of reading material for each child in order to create a fair balance between children who receive access to books outside of school and those who do not. Given that there are approximately 180 days in the school year, a child should be able to select within the classroom a new book to read each day. This averages to about seven books per student in each classroom library. School libraries should have a minimum of 20 books per child to enable children to take multiple books home at each visit. This figure also takes into consideration the needs of teachers to have access to quality trade books for literature-based instruction. In addition, it is recommended that one new book per student should be added to every classroom library, and two new books per child should be added to the school library collection each year to allow for the addition of important new titles and for the elimination of books that are no longer timely. Books and other literary materials must be updated annually. Worn and out-of-date materials must be replaced with timely and enriching new works.

Access means not only availability of books, but also time for reading them (Krashen, 1996). Regular periods need to be set aside in school for independent reading. Providing access to books also includes supplying a quiet, comfortable place to read. Another important part of access is librarians and teachers who know both books and children and who can make good recommendations that match the interests of children with the content of books.

What happens when literature is not readily available for student use?

Children become fluent readers when they have opportunities to practice reading. Without appropriate access to books, children will be taught to read, but will not develop the habit of reading. If schools fail to provide children with an opportunity to practice skills in the meaningful context of literature, substantial numbers of children will choose not to read for pleasure or for information on their own (Holdaway, 1979). Additionally, research has found a relation between the amount of time that children read for fun on their own and reading achievement (Greany, 1980; National Assessment of Educational Progress, 1996; Taylor, Frye, & Maruyama, 1990). Children in classrooms without literature collections read 50% less than children in classrooms with such collections (Morrow, 1998).

How can public libraries promote children's access to books?

Public libraries are necessary partners for the provision of children's access to books. Libraries often provide their own programs for children and parents to enhance the joy of reading and easy, free access to books. In these efforts, they can and often do collaborate with schools. Ramos & Krashen (1998) carried out a study that demonstrated the value of using the public library to provide children more access to books. In this study 104 children from homes that had few or no books visited their local libraries monthly. These children had limited access to print outside of the 30 minutes each week during library visits. When visiting the pub-

lic library, children were allowed to check out 10 books each. Some of these books were to increase the supply of literature in their classroom library, and some books were for taking to their homes. No assignments were made in regard to using these books; however, children read more, read with more ease, and were eager to return to the library. Surveys also indicated that children requested that their parents take them back to the library. This excitement creates a positive cycle in which wider reading helps increase reading ability and interest in books.

What are the implications for this position statement at the federal, state, district, and school levels?

Miller and Shontz (1993) found that schools that had up-to-date book collections in good condition often used advisory committees to study their current books status. Additionally, many of these schools received extra funding for online access, interactive video resources, and inter-library loans. Others used more of their federal and gift monies for books, and a higher percentage of these schools belong to networks.

The American Library Association has recommended that school libraries plan acquisition programs that are integrated with the instructional program of their school. Such a school program should decide what types of books are needed to help the school and the library achieve instructional goals. Librarians and teachers also need financial support from school budgets for book purchases and for school librarians to help with the use of the books (Guice, 1994).

Miller and Shontz (1993) suggest that the states, regional accrediting associations, and the National Center for Education Statistics research the deterioration of library collections to obtain more precise data. This would provide information to the states, the U.S. Department of Education, and Congress, and would encourage more financial support and programs to provide children access to print materials. State associations need to become aggressive on the issue of improving our libraries and should stress the contribution made by libraries to the quality of education for children (Miller & Shontz, 1993). Associations with vested interest in the education of children, such as the International Reading Association and the American Library Association, must continue to seek legislation from local and national government officials to provide adequate funding to keep classroom and school libraries current with quality literature.

Recommendations for teachers, librarians, and school administrators

• Request appropriate numbers of books for classrooms, school libraries, and public libraries.

• Inform parents and policy makers of the importance of access to books.

• Remind state and local policy makers of the need to allot funding for books.

Recommendations for researchers

• Survey homes in each community to determine children's access to books at home.

• Continue to study the benefits of access to books to document the issue and maintain its visibility among educators, policy makers, and the public.

It is easy to dismiss the issue addressed in this position statement. Providing access to books is not controversial, nor does it achieve the same high profile as other educational concerns that seem to be more pressing. However, among all the issues we face, few concern a more basic educational need: that our children have access to current, quality literature. We must never allow that need to go unaddressed.

REFERENCES

Calkins, L.M. (1996). *Lessons from a child.* Portsmouth, NH: Heinemann.

Elley, W.B., & Mangubhai, F. (1983). The impact of reading on second language reading. *Reading Research Quarterly, 19,* 53–67.

Fielding, L.G., Wilson, P.T., & Anderson, R.C. (1986). A new focus on free reading: The role of trade books in reading instruction. In T.E. Raphael (Ed.), *Contexts of school-based literacy* (pp. 149–160). New York: Random House.

Greaney V. (1980). Factors related to amount and type of leisure reading. *Reading Research Quarterly, 15,* 337–357.

Guice, S. (1994). *Access? Books, children, and literature-based curriculum in schools* (Report Series 1.13). (ERIC Document Reproduction Service No. ED 374 446)

Holdaway, D. (1979). *The foundations of literacy*. New York: Ashton Scholastic.

Ingham, J.L. (1981). *Books and reading development: The Bradford Book Flood Experiment*. Exeter, NH: Heinemann.

Irving, A. (1980). *Promoting voluntary reading for children and young people*. Paris: UNESCO.

Krashen, S. (1994). An answer to the literacy crisis: Free voluntary reading. *School Library Media Annual, 12*, 113–122.

Krashen, S. (1996). *Every person a reader*. Culver City, CA: Language Education Associates.

Miller, M.L., & Shontz, M. (1993). Expenditures for resources in school library media centers, FY 1991–1992. *School Library Journal, 39*(10), 26–36.

Morrow, L.M. (1983). Home and school correlates of early interest in literature. *Journal of Educational Research, 76*, 221–230.

Morrow, L.M. (1998). *Motivating lifelong voluntary readers*. Unpublished manuscript, New Brunswick, NJ: Rutgers University.

National Assessment of Educational Progress (NAEP). (1996). *Reading report card: Findings for the nation and the states*. Washington, DC: U.S. Department of Education, Office of Educational Research and Improvement.

Ramos, F., & Krashen, S. (1998). The impact of one trip to the public library: Making books available may be the best incentive for reading. *The Reading Teacher, 51*, 614–615.

Taylor, B.M., Frye, B., & Maruyama, J. (1990). Time spent reading and reading growth. *American Educational Research Journal, 27*, 351–362.

Related IRA Publications

Beyond Storybooks: Young Children and the Shared Book Experience
Judith Pollard Slaughter
1993

Children's Choices (annual booklist)
International Reading Association

Family Literacy Connections in Schools and Communities
Lesley Mandel Morrow, Editor
1995

Fostering the Love of Reading: The Affective Domain in Reading Education
Eugene H. Cramer and Marietta Castle, Editors
1993

Introducción a la literatura infantil y juvenil
Isabel Schon and Sarah Corona Berkin
1996

Magazines for Kids and Teens
Donald R. Stoll, Editor
1997

Research & Professional Resources in Children's Literature: Piecing a Patchwork Quilt
Kathy G. Short, Editor
1995

Teachers' Choices (annual booklist)
International Reading Association

Young Adults' Choices (annual booklist)
International Reading Association

Single copies of International Reading Association position statements are available in PDF format through the IRA Web site (www.reading.org/advocacy/policies). Or, send a self-addressed, stamped No. 10 envelope to International Reading Association, Attn. Dept. E.G., 800 Barksdale Road, PO Box 8139, Newark, DE 19714-8139, USA. To purchase multiple copies, visit the Association's Online Bookstore: bookstore.reading.org.

Information on International Reading Association "Choices" booklists

Among the most popular features of the International Reading Association's print journals *The Reading Teacher* and the *Journal of Adolescent & Adult Literacy* are the annual "Choices" booklists.

The Children's Choices project is cosponsored by the International Reading Association and the Children's Book Council, and the booklist appears each year in the October issue of *The Reading Teacher*. The list includes brief reviews of approximately 100 titles, each of which has been recommended by the children themselves. Each year 10,000 school children from different regions of the United States read and vote on the newly published children's books they like best. This list is designed for use not only by teachers, librarians, administrators, and booksellers, but also by parents, caregivers, and everyone who wishes to encourage young people to read for pleasure.

Each year the International Reading Association's Teachers' Choices project identifies approximately 30 outstanding U.S. trade books for children and adolescents that teachers find to be exceptional in curriculum use. Parents also will find books from the Teachers' Choices list good for reading aloud at home.

The annotated booklist, which appears in the November issue of *The Reading Teacher*, is accomplished through a national field test of more than 300 newly published books submitted by U.S. trade book publishers.

Young Adults' Choices, a list that appears in the November issue of the *Journal of Adolescent & Adult Literacy*, provides descriptions of approximately 30 books selected by teams of teenage reviewers from five different regions of the United States. The goals of the project are to encourage young people to read; to make teens, teachers, librarians, and parents aware of new literature for young adults; and to provide middle school and secondary school students with an opportunity to voice their opinions about books being written for them.

The Choices booklists are available in PDF format through the International Reading Association Web site (www.

reading.org/choices). Copies also may be requested by sending a 9"×12" self-addressed stamped envelope plus $1.00 postage and handling for each list to International Reading Association, 800 Barksdale Road, PO Box 8139, Newark, DE 19714-8139.